ART SEPT. 1998

Sell Yourself !

■

Sell Yourself!

Persuasive Tactics to Boost Your Image

■

POLLY BIRD

the Institute
of Management

PITMAN PUBLISHING

PITMAN PUBLISHING
128 Long Acre, London WC2E 9AN

A Division of Longman Group Limited

First published in Great Britain 1994

Reprinted 1994 (twice)

A CIP catalogue record for this book can be obtained
from the British Library.

ISBN 0 273 60331 0 (Paperback)
ISBN 0 273 60747 2 (Cased)

Photoset in Linotron Century Schoolbook by
Northern Phototypesetting Co. Ltd., Bolton
Printed and bound in Great Britain
by Bell and Bain Ltd, Glasgow

*The Publishers' policy is to use paper manufactured
from sustainable forests.*

To James, Paul and Rebecca, with love

Contents

■

Acknowledgements

■

I am grateful to the following people who agreed to be interviewed for this book: Jane Ageros of Abbey National, Hilary Perkins, Blackett Ditchburn of Prudential Corporation, Joy King of Manweb, Colin D. Duncan of BNFL, Chris Casburn of Mercury Communications and Barry S. Hyman of Marks and Spencer.

Once again my thanks go to my agent Teresa Chris and to David Crosby and his colleagues at Pitman.

Finally I thank my husband, Jon, and my children James, Paul and Rebecca for their patience with me while this book was being written.

Polly Bird, Chester, 1993

Introduction

∎

You know the work you do is valuable. But do you ever feel that it is unappreciated by your colleagues and customers? Do you wish that your job had a better image?

Dentists, for example, think that their customers undervalue them. Their clients dread their visits and leave thinking 'thank goodness that's over!' But my dentist always greets me with a cheerful smile and asks about my family. I warm to her as an individual and this gives me more confidence in her work. I almost look forward to my next visit.

If you ever feel that the services, skills or product *you* offer in your work environment are undervalued by the general public, your customers, clients, colleagues or employees, then take heart. There are ways to improve the image of what you have to offer and to make it more attractive to them, so that the image you project to particular groups of people becomes the image of the work you do or the business you run. To do this you must become your own publicist by creating a suitable image of yourself, to everyone who comes into contact with you in your work – your colleagues, employees, superiors, customers, clients and the general public. Then, like the dentist's patients, your customers will leave thinking 'what a nice person that is!' instead of dreading their next visit. In short, you must sell yourself and not your work. The image you project can be crucial to the success or failure of your business. It may even be more important than the worth of what you have to offer, in terms of price, value and satisfaction. And once the image of your organisation has improved your job prospects will be enhanced. Self-promotion leads to improved business which leads to improved job prospects.

Although you may have only one message that you wish to promote, for example in the case of the dentist that you care for teeth well, you may need to do this by presenting a different image to different people. The dentist will wish to present a caring and reliable face to customers and an efficient and cost-effective face to his accountant. Many people do this naturally. Many more are confused about how a personal image can be projected to the world outside. Others like the idea of projecting a changed image of themselves but are scared of trying it out.

Your image and what you do at work go hand in hand. But let us be clear what we mean by the term. Your image is the total view that other people have of you. It will include how you present your ideas to people, how you behave in company, how you dress, how you speak, what you say and what you do. This personal image will in turn become the image of your organisation and job and how other people will remember it.

The more effective an organisation wishes to be, the more it must cultivate the goodwill not only of its employees but also of the public at large. This is best done by promoting the images of individuals. Although an organisation may have a corporate image, or a job may be seen by clients in terms of all similar work, a client's reaction to any particular organisation is often coloured by his or her reaction to an individual such as a receptionist, manager, or in the case of professions, the professional him or herself. Therefore you and every other member of your staff is an individual public relations officer for the business. Everyone needs to be made to understand that by presenting a good image of themselves for the sake of the firm they are improving the firm's image, and that success in this will lead to improved prospects for all employees. Promoting individuals can be done by direct presentation of your image or, in the case of the general public, by means of the media, whether radio, television or the press.

Before you can change your image you need to know what aspect of your work situation you are trying to promote. Having established that, you need to learn how to promote your new image to others. This book will take you through these stages so that you will have a thorough grounding in promoting your image to enhance the standing of your work.

Do not be afraid of pushing yourself forward. Promoting yourself, and therefore your work, is not difficult. The techniques are straightforward and easily learnt and applied. Reading this book will help you change your image for the better. By the end of the book I will have turned you from an image 'mouse' into a promotional 'lion'. And you and your business will benefit.

How to use this book

This is a book to be used and not simply read. Each chapter will provide you with a series of learning points. These are the important ideas and techniques you need to remember in order to improve your image and promote it successfully. You will find these incorporated into a ten-day action plan. By following the plan and putting these points into operation you will make quick and visible progress in promoting your chosen image.

Although the plan can be carried out in ten consecutive days, you may find it easier to put it into effect on one day each week or month. This will give you the time between to consolidate what you have learnt and to put it into practice. The learning checklists will remind you of the important lessons to be learnt from each chapter. Once you have started the ten-day plan you can use the checklists to look back on as a quick guide and a reminder of follow-up action.

Interviews with the experts

Seven of the chapters include interviews about image with senior managers from major companies. The interviews are self-contained and are not intended to endorse the chapters in which they appear. I hope that reading these interviews and the rest of this book will start you thinking creatively about your own image.

You and your image

Who do you want to be? How do you want others to view you and your work? Can changing your individual image improve your business? Does your image really affect your clients? You may have pondered these questions from time to time for a variety of reasons. You may have seen less able colleagues promoted over you; you may have felt that clients have not reacted as positively to your business and work as you might have expected; you may feel your job is undervalued by your bosses and customers; you may simply want to make the most of yourself to improve your job prospects. Whatever the reason for improving your image, this book will tell you how to go about it in the most effective way.

Everyone can improve their image and that of their work and business. The trick is to persuade other people to see you as you want to be seen. To do this you have to understand how image works and what it is. Then you can use this knowledge to improve your own image.

What image is

Before you start to change your image you must understand what it is. Your image is the perception people have of you. It is the total picture of yourself that you present to people. It includes how you look, speak, dress and act; your skills, your attitudes, posture and body language; your accessories and your surroundings and the company you keep.

POINTS OF VIEW

Like your personality there can be many facets to your image. There will be the image you portray when relaxing at home with friends, the image you portray to your mother-in-law, the image your portray to your enemies and the image you portray at work.

Although all these may be different they are all based on the one reality – you. They are simply different viewpoints of one personality. So portraying an image is not being dishonest; it is presenting one facet of yourself to the world. If you try to change your personality completely, or do or say things which deep down you hate, then you will be behaving dishonestly and will be found out. So whatever image you want or need to portray to the world has to be rooted in yourself.

FIRST TIME LUCKY

2

In spite of the fact that many different things go to make up your total image, most people will make a judgement about you in the first three minutes of meeting you and will only modify this a little as they get to know you. With customers you may meet only once you can see that this first image of you will be the abiding one and the one that will colour how they perceive you, your job and your company afterwards. It is important, therefore, not only to decide what image you want to portray of yourself and your work but also to be consistent in presenting it. It is no good wanting to be seen as a smart go-getting manager if you sometimes turn up to meet a client wearing jeans and with an offhand attitude. You may think that once in a while it won't matter but it will. Word will get around and people will form expectations of you before they meet you. If they expect to meet an off-putting and lazy person, even your 'go-getter' style won't budge them from that preformed opinion. So you need to decide on your image and make it become a natural part of you.

Discover who you are

You cannot start to alter your image until you know who you

are and what your present image is. It is a rare person who can sit down and immediately write an accurate description of themselves. You may think of yourself in entirely negative or entirely positive terms. This is self-deluding and will not help you. You must be prepared to look at yourself in an honest way.

DIFFERENCES BETWEEN HOW YOU ARE AND HOW OTHERS SEE YOU

You may think that you know yourself very well. But there can be a big difference between how you think you present yourself and how others see you. You may see yourself as confident and cheerful; other people may see you as brash and self-satisfied. You may think yourself shy and cowardly; other people may see you as a good listener and sensible.

3

WHAT OTHERS THINK OF YOU NOW

It is important to find out what people think of you now. You cannot begin to decide what image you want to put across to other people or how you want to change your present image unless you know how others see you at the moment. These 'others' in your work life will include different groups of people: your colleagues, bosses, clients, visitors. Although you need a coherent image you may need to present yourself in a slightly different way to these different groups, so that you emphasise different aspects of your image.

HOW TO FIND OUT

The only way to find out how others see you is to ask them. This can be upsetting or useless if you do not do this carefully. If your colleagues and friends see you only in negative terms or your customers only come back to you with praise you will get a distorted view of yourself. So your quest needs to be done in two stages. First collect the comments and then analyse them so that you arrive at an overall picture.

SELF ANALYSIS

First of all provide yourself with several large sheets of paper. List a different group of people on each one e.g. clients on one and colleagues on another. Then ask these people for their honest comments and put them on the relevant sheet. Do not attempt any analysis of them at this stage, especially if they all appear to be negative. Include a sheet of comments from relatives and friends as well, because these people see you out of a work environment and can round out the picture of yourself.

If you are shy about asking people you could ask them to write down comments in a spare moment or perhaps during a lunch hour. Try not to ask them during work when they will be busy and not interested in doing this for you. Do not get upset at some of the comments if they are negative and do not take silly comments too seriously (there are always jokers). Put the sheets aside.

Now get another sheet and head it 'ME'. On it write down all the things you think about yourself. Do not be entirely negative. Everyone has good points. Try to be honest and admit you've got some. For example, part of your list might read:

- Bad timekeeper
- Good at giving presentations
- Talk too much at meetings
- Get on well with subordinates

Do not try to separate good from bad points at this point. Just write down everything.

QUESTIONNAIRE

Fill in the questionnaire opposite to help you gauge your personality type. Tick one of the boxes for each question. Add up the number of ticks in each column to find out what kind of personality you have.

WHAT THE RESULTS MEAN

Mostly No. You are the shy, retiring type who would rather

	No	Sometimes	Yes
1 Do I work well on my own?			✓
2 Am I well-organised?			✓
3 Can I cope with stress?			✓
4 Do I enjoy meeting people?	✓		✓
5 Do I take the lead in meetings?	✓		
6 Do I need a routine?			✓
7 Have I any interests outside work?			✓
8 Do I read newspapers regularly?		✓	
9 Do I get upset when I am criticised?		✓	
10 Do I welcome new projects?			✓
11 Do I want to learn new skills?			✓
12 Do I enjoy teamwork			✓
13 Do I take care with my clothes?			✓
14 Am I ambitious?			✓
15 Do I get on with my colleagues?			✓
16 Have I done any public speaking?	✓		
17 Do I work well under pressure?			✓
18 Am I adaptable?			✓
19 Do I fear the unknown?		✓	
20 Do people listen to my ideas?			✓
21 Do people remember my name?		✓	

5

work quietly in a corner than join in with a team effort. You are good at your job but lack the communication skills necessary to bring your talents to the notice of the people who matter. You prefer to be led, rather than lead, and shy away from any kind of public speaking. You tend to feel stressful if you have to take on new work and you do not volunteer to take on new projects. You are aware that you are not projecting the right image but are not sure what to do about it.

You need to take a good look at what training is available and work on becoming more approachable and outspoken. This book will tell you how to start to discover your strengths and then capitalise on them.

Mostly Sometimes. You have no objection to working in a team but find your contributions get passed over. You take part in social activities at work and get on well with your colleagues but are nervous of your boss. You sometimes find that your staff take their problems to someone else. Customers like you but can never remember your name. You want to improve your image but are unsure how to go about it.

This book will build on your strengths and help you to make that transition from being almost the right person in the right place to having a starring image in your company.

Mostly Yes. You are confident and organised and have your eye on the future. You keep a sharp eye on what the company will need and take regular training in useful subjects. You read widely in your own speciality as well as keeping up with national and local news. You are well liked and regarded and have every expectation of making it to the top.

Beware of over-confidence. There are other people working towards the same goals who may step in before you (especially when they have read this book!). Use this book to keep one jump ahead of the crowd and to sharpen up your image for the competitive market place.

Understanding your present image

One way of understanding what your present image is to compare your strengths and weaknesses so that you can see where you need to make changes.

You need to be honest about this. It is better to write 'I am good at preparing talks for other people but don't like giving them myself' rather than 'I am no good at talks'. The first version tells you that you are good at basic written communication skills, good enough in fact for other people to rely on you to write their speeches for them. You only lack the skill of giving the talk yourself and that is something that can be learnt. So do not be negative, but on the other hand do not overpraise yourself.

Now write down your strengths and weaknesses in two columns (everyone has lots of both!). Then see if any contradict each other. For instance, under strength you might have written 'I get on well with people' and later under weakness put 'I am shy'. Decide which version is nearer the truth or whether you can modify one of the remarks.

A DIFFERENT VIEW

When you have your list look at it again and try and see your assessment from other people's point of view. Ask a friend or colleague to go over it with you, and see what they make of it. You may have written 'I am good at work and get on with it quietly'. Other people might interpret that trait as 'she is self-contained and never communicates with colleagues if she can help it'. Or you might have written 'I am hopeless at writing reports because I always think of too many things to go in them', which might be seen as 'he is always full of good ideas and just needs to harness them more'.

7

WHAT CHANGES ARE NEEDED?

With your comments and lists in front of you mark in red any changes that you can make. Do this by looking at each sentence in turn and asking yourself 'what do I need to do to improve? How can I make the change?'.

With the comment 'I am good at writing reports but not good at giving them myself' you would write 'I need to learn how to improve my oral communication skills and public speaking skills. I can do this by signing up for the company three-day course on public speaking skills. I can volunteer to give a short talk to my local history society and I can practise giving a talk by giving it to a friend or in front of the mirror. I can record my voice so that I can hear how I sound.' If you do this for each comment you will have a comprehensive list of changes to make and ideas to follow up. If you are completely stuck for ideas about how to improve, don't despair. This is what this book will help you with. Use the following questionnaire to help you decide what changes to make. For each comment on yourself ask yourself:

1 Is this a strength or a weakness?

2 If this is a strength, can I improve on it?

3 If this is a weakness, what do I need to change?

4 What new skills do I need?

5 What training do I need?

6 Is the training easily available?

7 Will the company train me in this?

8 Do I need more information?

9 Where can I get the information?

10 Are there any people I know who can help me or advise me?

11 Will changes require extensive training or is it something I can teach myself?

Rewrite your list under basic headings:

- written communication skills
- oral communication skills
- dress improvement
- job training
- body changes (hair, make up, etc)
- interpersonal skills
- assertiveness training

By filling in a chart like this you will be able to see which aspect of your image needs the most work.

Ready, steady, go!

This book contains a ten-day plan for you to follow. It will give you practical pointers to ways of improving your image. You may not need to do everything, or you may feel that you need to give your image a complete overhaul. Don't start the plan until you have completed the questionnaires in this chapter and made the self-analysis lists. You need to know where you are starting from before you can work out where to go!

Before you start buy a large notebook. Copy your lists on to alternative left-hand pages. On the right-hand page write down what you have achieved for each comment on the list after each day of the plan. You will soon see how much you have progressed and what you need to learn. Use the notebook as an image diary. Besides comments on your plan write down useful things that you learn. Make notes about what impressed you in other people or the name of a particularly useful book. When you have finished this book and worked through the plan you will end up with a personal guide to your image as well as a permanent personal image reference book.

At the beginning of the book paste a picture of yourself in your work clothes. Write underneath all the things you want to achieve with your image. At the back of the book after you have finished the plan paste an up-to-date picture and a list of the things you have achieved! A permanent confidence booster!

9

LEARNING POINTS CHECKLIST

1 Be honest about your strengths and weaknesses

2 Do not be entirely negative about yourself

3 Remember other people may see your weaknesses as strengths and vice versa

4 Ask friends and colleagues to help you with your self-analysis

5 Answer the questionnaires to find out what your image is now

6 Be positive about what changes you can make

7 Find out whether you can get image training at work

8 Everyone can change their image

9 Remember you don't have to change everything at once

10 Buy a notebook to record your image progress

First choices

You can work hard at improving your image but unless you are sure who you are trying to impress the work will be wasted. In the same way that many people like ice-cream but not everyone likes strawberry flavour, so many people will like some aspects of your image but not others. Should you try to impress everyone in a general way or tailor your image to groups of people who are most important to you? Senior managers are generally agreed that your image has to be based on your true self. It is no good presenting an unrealistic and unnatural persona to everyone you meet. The basics of a good image for any group of people you meet is that they should be meeting the real you and not some made-up version.

Having said that, it should be obvious that you cannot behave in all situations and to all people the same way. How you behave to your colleagues when you are going about your daily business may not be quite the same as how you behave to your superiors when you are negotiating an increase in salary. So first of all you must decide what group of people you are trying to impress. Then you need to discover what impresses you about other people. Role models have their uses and it is sensible to work out what impresses you in other people and see if you can adapt that to your own image. Not only do you need to adapt your personal image to different groups of people but you also need to deduce what aspect of your work you are promoting and to whom. Will that make a difference to how you present yourself? Your individual image has many facets. You need to discover your strengths so that you can capitalise on them.

This chapter will show you how to work out who you are trying to impress and will help you discover what impresses you in other people. You will discover how to work out what aspect of your work situation you are trying to promote and to whom, and how to capitalise on your strengths. At the end of this chapter you will find day one of your action plan to help you turn your image into reality.

Define your groups

Your image needs to be suitable and effective for many different groups of people. In the work situation there are a variety of important groups to consider. These can include:

- customers and clients
- colleagues
- your work superiors
- your staff
- advertisers
- suppliers
- publicity department
- communications department
- the media
- the general public
- accountant

These are the groups of people who will probably figure largely in your work life and who may need a different part of your image to be projected at them. But your work is also affected by your home life and so you will need to take into account the reactions of:

- your partner
- your children
- your relatives
- your friends

If your image at work is wildly at variance with your image at home then this will cause you and your family pain. You will feel stressed at having to project two quite dissimilar images and your family will not understand how the person they thought they knew had so drastically changed. It is therefore important that you discuss any major changes you make with your family and friends so that you do not suddenly appear changed for no reason. And it is all the more important that your work image is based strongly on the best bits of your true personality.

How do other people impress you?

It is an unnerving thought that your image needs changing. You will probably feel completely blank about how to do it and what you need to change.

Start from what you can observe yourself. There are probably other people at work or whom you meet in the course of your job that impress you both by their attitude to work and how they react to you and your colleagues. They leave you feeling pleased with yourself, satisfied that any transaction or meeting was worthwhile, whatever the outcome, and generally present themselves as pleasant and trustworthy. Do these people have attributes which you particularly admire? Consider the following and then make your own list:

- do they have a particular character trait that you admire?
- is there a style of dress which impresses you?
- what is it about their speech and mannerisms that attracts you?
- how do they make you feel that you trust them?
- what is their attitude to work?
- what are their qualifications?
- what kind of people do they associate with?
- how do they spend their spare time?

You will not admire all these things in all people. Jot down the things that impress you in your role models and then see what characteristics they have in common. You will have different lists for different people. But your list in common may include, for example:

- dress is always very neat and clean
- shoes always shined
- personal hygiene good and hair always clean and tidy
- straightforward in conversation
- reliable
- honest
- good timekeeper
- good listener
- work always done and to high standard
- takes managerial courses in own time
- spends weekend with family
- effective in argument
- gets their own way
- enthusiastic about work

13

Your list will be different to mine but I suspect that honesty, reliability, good dress and hygiene and enthusiasm will be on everybody's list.

HOW DID THEY DO IT?

Now that you know what impresses you in other people you need to find out *how* they impressed you. Let's take the simple example of dress. You noticed in several of your role models that they were neat and clean in their dress. What gives you that impression? You may come up with:

- hair always well cut and tidy. There is never any dandruff on the collar
- personal hygiene always good. Uses anti-perspirant deodorant and keeps nails cut. Always seems to have just had a shower
- clothes are classic but not out-dated. Wears a plain leather watchstrap and one gold ring. Wears plain ear studs and simple brooch. New shirt every day. Or, if you aspire to a different style; wears striped shirt and red braces but shirt is

always tucked in and freshly ironed. Or, wears large gold earrings and tapered trousers
- has at least two pairs of glasses in different frames

You can do a different list for each of the characteristics you have noted in common. Once you have identified similar ways and means for each characteristic you can start to put it into practice. Again using dress as an example, you can:

- get your hair cut regularly
- be more particular about your personal hygiene and use anti-perspirant deodorants
- have a daily bath or shower
- wear a clean, ironed shirt daily. Iron five at the beginning of the week or a fresh one each night
- shine your shoes daily (something lots of people omit)
- keep your jewellery (men and women) to something simple and little of it. In certain work situations a lot of jewellery can be dangerous
- buy a few good quality clothes rather than lots of cheap ones and keep them laundered and repaired
- trim nails weekly

For personality your list might read:

- think before you speak
- don't gabble
- listen to other people
- smile more
- make intelligent small talk – read a broadsheet paper daily
- be honest
- firm handshake

Put these ideas into practice straight away.

Which part of your work for which people?

All of your work is important to you. But only parts of it are important to other people. If you want your work to be valued

14

then you have to make sure that you are presenting to the different groups of people the aspect of it which most interests them.

Your senior may well be interested in all aspects of your work because he or she has to have an overall view of what you are doing and how it fits into the company. But other people will be looking for a different emphasis. For example, your colleagues may be dealing with different parts of a project you are working on. So Peter may be concentrating on the presentation to clients and Sally may be working on the financial plan. How you present your work to them will differ slightly.

You cannot be flippant about finance which plays an underlying vital role in any project. So Sally will want to see that you are taking it seriously, both when giving advice and in listening to what she has to say. She will want to see that you have done your work on that side of the project so that she is not kept waiting for you to provide her with vital facts and figures. In short, you must present a reliable, serious and supportive image. For Peter who is concentrating on the clients you will need to present a more outward facing image, of someone who knows the kind of problems he will face when meeting clients, and who can tell him what to do to make the presentation less nerve-wracking. So you will need to be confident and encouraging.

It is not a question of acting in a way which is completely foreign to your nature but a question of drawing out that aspect of your personality which is needed at the time. Your image must be suitable and appropriate not only for the occasion but the person. You must also present the right aspect of your work. When you meet your boss you may need to project reliability and confidence not only in your work overall but also bringing out particular work themes. For example, you may want to encourage your boss to consider you for promotion, so you would project the reliable, honest, enthusiastic and energetic part of your image. You would concentrate on discussing and promoting the work which you would want to do in your new job. If it is a job that needs someone who has a sound financial sense and is willing to work long hours then you will emphasise that aspect of your image. The financial part of the

15

project will be up to date and you will not go in seemingly casual about the whole thing.

Different images for different people

It may be more important that you project a different image to different people. You would not, I am sure, project the same image to your home partner as to your colleagues. Sometimes people have to work at home but it is unusual to project the same image in both places. The work may be the same but the situation is different. You would expect the work at home to be done in shirtsleeves, perhaps, in relaxing surroundings. At work a more formal attitude may be required and you would talk to your colleagues in a more formal way.

Most people automatically adjust their image to the person they are speaking to. Some do so to the extent of mimicking the other person's accent. Most are unaware that they do this so this is something you should stop if you find yourself doing it, as most people find it irritating, not flattering. Children learn this early on when they have one language for school, one language for home, and yet another for their friends.

In the same way you will find yourself adjusting the way you react to people according to the situation. Take time to think about how you adjust to different situations and then work out how you can improve this. For instance, if you find that when you meet clients you always talk more formally and sit up straighter you could emphasise this by dressing more formally.

How to capitalise on your strengths

On your worst days you will probably think that you have no redeeming aspects to your image at all. You may say 'I never dress right for any situation, I am nervous when I meet clients, can't make a presentation properly, talk too much when I see my boss, am considered untrustworthy and lazy and nobody likes me'. We all feel like that sometimes, but quite frankly it can't really be true or you wouldn't be a manager.

You must start by discovering what your strengths are so that you can make them work for you. The more you concentrate on your strengths the quicker your weaknesses will be eliminated or will fade away. Make a positive list of your strengths in the work situation such as:

- I always get my work done on time
- my staff find me easy to talk to
- my colleagues ask me for advice
- I'm a good listener
- I'm an expert on my subject
- I like meeting clients
- people laugh at my jokes

How can you make your strengths work for you? How can you use them to boost your image? Let us look at the above imaginary list.

1. I always get my work done on time. This is an aspect of your image which will appeal to a wide range of people. Your boss will appreciate a member of staff who is reliable. Your colleagues will appreciate not being held up by you. And clients will trust you to deliver on time. You can use this to boost your image with these people. You can tell clients 'I have a reputation for delivering on time and to budget. Ask other clients'. A reputation for reliability is a great asset in business.

2. My staff find me easy to talk to. Use this to encourage feedback at departmental meetings and team meetings. If other people can see that your staff are not afraid to talk openly to and in front of you and listen to your advice this will boost your image with other people in the workplace. Word would certainly get round quickly if your staff did not find you easy to communicate with. Equally a sympathetic but fair manager is viewed with respect by everyone.

3. My colleagues ask me for advice. Again encourage this questioning at meetings where other members of the company attend.

4. I'm a good listener. You may feel you are too quiet, but a good listener is a rare commodity. But listen carefully. Do not just sit there and nod. Make comments which show that you have understood what the speaker is getting at, and use the information and act on it. If people see that you have not only listened but *absorbed* what they have been saying your image will receive a great boost.

5. I'm an expert on my subject. If you know it well enough to have written papers on it then try writing articles for the house journal or appropriate trade paper, in order to spread your image wider. Do not be stingy with your expertise. Be generous in teaching others what you know and helping them with their work. You image will improve by doing so. Somebody who has a reputation for keeping to him or herself knowledge which could help other people in the company will be viewed as untrustworthy and uncooperative. Someone who is generous with information and help has a strength of character and shows confidence in their own ability. And that image of confidence is what you want others to perceive.

6. I like meeting clients. Your image will improve if you are willing to take on more of this face-to-face contact. Not everyone is good at it.

7. People laugh at my jokes. You may feel that comments like this on your own list hardly count as strengths. But consider your humour. Is it clean and funny, or smutty and the sort of humour that colleagues laugh at behind their hands? If it is the former then you have a valuable asset. You are not only a good worker but fun to be with and that is a great image booster. Fun people attract people. That doesn't mean that you should be frivolous about your work, because that will have a counter-effect. But someone who can lightly amuse in the breaks of a lengthy meeting will be popular. Don't overdo it, though.

LEARNING POINTS CHECKLIST

1 Define which groups you relate to at work

2 Notice what impresses you about other people

3 Remember that your image is an aspect of your personality

4 Capitalise on your strengths

5 Don't be too negative about yourself

6 Make your strengths work for you

7 Let your weaknesses fade away

8 Adjust your image to different groups

9 Discuss your image changes with family and friends

10 Start your action plan today!

DAY ONE ACTION PLAN

Before you can change your image you need to assess it. In your notebook make a list of all the people you need to impress with your image. Leave several lines beneath each name, then underneath each write what you think they look for in someone's image.

Now you are ready to discover what impresses you in other people. On another page write down the names of people you know who impress you and whose image you would like to emulate in some aspect or other. Leave several lines underneath each one and write there the characteristics that impress you.

Your third list is probably the most important. Here write down the things that these role model people have in common. What aspects of their image do they all display in common? These aspects are the ones that are most important to join in the way they present themselves. The characteristics they have in common are obviously the most important aspects of your role models for him to emulate. Write down at least three ways that you can change your image to achieve those characteristics. Now write down your strengths. Be honest and positive! Everyone has strengths. Write down three ways you can accentuate them.

It is no good just writing lists, however much fun it is. Now you have to work on them. You can start with the following:

1 Make sure that you are clean and tidy for work tomorrow

2 Make a date in your diary to get your hair cut

3 Have a shower

4 Make sure your clothes are clean, ironed and repaired

5 Make a date in your diary to go shopping for one classic and stylish piece of clothing for work

6 Assess your jewellery. Can you dispense with some of it for work?

7 Put one of your role models' attributes into action tomorrow – maybe smile more, show enthusiasm for your work, listen more carefully to colleagues?

Who chooses your style?

The decision to make changes to your image is hard. One of the most difficult things about it is to decide who is going to dictate your image and by how much.

Many companies do have, if not rules about image, at least a set of values which they expect their work force to follow. How far should you let your image be dictated to by those above you? Will it affect your rise in the company if you don't toe the line? Are there unwritten rules you should follow? And how do you find out what the management image is? Is it the same for everyone or do different departments have different images? Once you have discovered the answers to these questions then you need to look at how far you want to change your image and how you can do so.

This chapter will help you decide how much your boss should dictate your image, how far you want your image to change and how to set about changing it. At the end of the chapter will be day two of the ten-day action plan.

Who chooses, you or your boss?

Most large organisations have a company style, if not in dress then certainly in the way that members are expected to behave towards their colleagues and their clients. If you want to progress in a company with definite terms of reference as far as personal image is concerned, you would be foolish to ignore this entirely.

If everyone else in the company turns up to work in classic suits and you turn up in jeans you *may* be viewed as the company eccentric, but more likely you will be expected to

conform or gently encouraged to look elsewhere for employ-
ment. Some people think that if a person is brilliant at their job
they can ignore the general rule and do what they like. But that
is to ignore one important point. However brilliant you are,
unless you can communicate those ideas to your colleagues,
clients, bosses and the general public, your brilliance is wasted,
your excellent work cannot progress. And communication is
made easier by a certain conformity in the way you dress and
speak and behave.

Another problem is that certain people are in jobs which
carry with them certain baggage as to the expectations of the
general public. For instance, accountants are supposed always
to be dressed in suits and to be boring, the creative team are
flamboyant in dress and character, and many people still
assume that poets work alone in attics! Remember too that
there may be an 'internal' style by which the various professions or managers recognise each other but which could be
off-putting to clients. For example, pony-tails for men, three
days' growth of beard for communications people or an exotic
way of dress for a woman, may signal to other communications
managers that you belong to the same job. But it may take a
client several meetings to realise that such people are actually
good at their jobs because they will be suspicious of the way
they look.

This may seem unfair but to get on in any profession and to
get people to value your job you want to give the general public
every opportunity to confirm a good opinion of you and your
work and as soon as possible. If it takes your client or an
interested bystander several meetings before they can trust
you to do the job or appreciate your value then you are not
making a good impression and may lose business. You do not
want anyone to be able to say 'I would have liked to do business
with you, but you weren't quite what I expected.'

SO WHO CHOOSES?

Having looked at all these problems of expectation from the
company or the general public, who decides your image? You
should obviously try to conform, to a certain extent. To do

otherwise will simply encourage your superiors to see you as a misfit who should be moved on or sidelined. But that does not mean that you cannot alter your image to your own specifications within the main framework.

For example, if the ethos of the firm is one of smart dress, customer service and hard work you are hardly going to win points by turning up scruffy, being offhand to clients or lazy. But you can improve on this as an individual by the way you show enthusiasm for your work, by tempering smart dress with personal accessories, by an individual style in ensuring good customer relations (maybe they like you because they like your sense of humour?)

Managerial style, fact or fiction?

Although company and client expectations may dictate a certain managerial style, this can vary not only from company to company, profession to profession, but also individual to individual. Take, for example, Sir John Harvey-Jones on the one hand and his successor at ICI, Sir Denys Henderson, on the other. Harvey-Jones plays on his eccentric 'break the rules' image by wearing clashing shirts and ties and long hair. His slightly unkempt appearance and brash style makes him unmistakable in a profession where conformity is usual. Because he is a brilliant communicator he can afford to allow his image to be different. Sir Denys Henderson has a more conformist style. He does not stand out as unusual but nevertheless his expertise makes him equally as effective.

23

Are there assets in common here which you should be following as far as managerial style goes? Yes, certain things should be at the root of any good managerial image:

- expertise at the job
- reliability
- enthusiasm for the job
- generosity in sharing your expertise
- suitable attire
- a pleasant manner

- ability to get on with others
- ability to inspire others
- ability to get things done

These are the basics of any good managerial style, and should be what you do anyway. If you don't, then now is the time to take yourself in hand and ensure that these qualities are worked on.

WHERE DO YOU FIT IN?

To find out what you need to improve, ask yourself these questions:

1 How expert am I at my job? Is there any extra training or research I could do to improve my expertise?

2 Am I consistently reliable? Is there any way I can improve this?

3 Do I always show enthusiasm for the job or do I let dissatisfaction show to my clients?

4 Am I happy to share my knowledge? Am I doing as much as I can to help train others and pass on my wisdom?

5 Is my attire suitable for my role or do I deliberately ignore expected standards of dress?

6 Do I have a pleasant personal manner or do people find me off-putting or boring? Are there mannerisms I can eliminate or improve on?

7 Do I get on with other people or do I try to avoid them? What steps can I take to overcome this ?

8 Do other people, such as my team, seem inspired by me or do they carry on independently of me?

When you have answered these questions you will get a good idea of how you fit into the management image and what aspects of it you deviate from.

Other styles

Let's take a lighthearted look at other styles you might want to aspire to. See if you recognise anyone you know!

THE FLAMBOYANT

This one comes in two types – the flashy executive and the creative type.

The flashy executives wear the traditional suits but their accessories are brightly coloured or slightly over the top. Men wear plain shirts but their ties are gaudy and they may sport a coloured handkerchief. Their hair is slightly longer than normal. The women wear bright dresses and exotic jewellery. Both sexes are outspoken, hail-fellow-well-met and exude energy and enthusiasm – sometimes over-enthusiasm, their colleagues think.

The creative type can be spotted from a hundred paces. Long hair is de rigueur, usually in a pony-tail. Glasses if worn are coloured with round or trendy shaped lenses. Red braces and striped shirts or huge dangly earrings and wide trousers. A laid-back manner and lots of buzz words finish the look.

25

THE CLASSIC

Well-tailored suits, understated accessories and jewellery and a calm, measured approach to their work make a classic look manager. Their clothes are good quality and bought to last. They exude confidence and move smoothly through the everyday life of the office.

THE SPECIALIST

This can include anyone from the scientist to the engineer, from the artist to the computer whiz kid. What these all have in common is a dedication to their work which precludes any attention to their appearance or manner. Clothes are scruffy, hair is unkempt, their manner and presentation techniques leave a lot to be desired. They can talk for hours in detail on their favourite subject – their work – but have no small talk. They are tolerated for their genius rather than admired for themselves.

THE LISTENER

These types of managers are the ones you hardly notice. They wear nothing distinctive and rarely make themselves conspicuous in the office. The work gets done by their team efficiently and they are always there to listen to ideas, complaints and comments. Their quiet authority is a stabilising influence in an uncertain world and whereas they themselves may not progress rapidly their staff do.

Choosing your image

When you come to think about your own image you need to have a clear set of objectives. Just picking an image at random may work for a short while but the long-term effects will elude you or be unfavourable. You need to pick an image which not only fits in with your own character but also with your long-term career aims as well as the ethos of your company. You will need to consider the following:

- character – are you shy, extrovert, cheerful or gloomy?
- attributes – are you a good listener, do you get things done, do people ask you for advice?
- dress – do you prefer a formal way of dressing or do you like a bit of colour in your dress?
- the company ethos – is there a set of unspoken rules or values about behaviour and dress that you need to take into consideration?
- expectations of others – is your job one which immediately raises expectations in the minds of others?
- willingness to learn – are you willing to undergo training or be advised about your image or your job?
- temperament – are you doing a job to which you are temperamentally suited (e.g. why continue as a computer programmer if you hate spending all day at a desk?)
- commitment – do you care about your job, your organisation, your colleagues, your image?

Clearly it is sensible and will be far more effective if you adapt and tailor your image to take account of your own personality and leanings. It is soon obvious to people when somebody is trying to project an image that is out of character. That does not mean that you can not alter your image, only that you should adapt it within the bounds of your own self in order to have the most impact. A shy person who suddenly starts telling blue jokes not only feels embarrassed but projects that embarrassment to the audience.

DRESS TO IMPRESS

Coupled with temperament and character is dress, the outward sign of your image. The usual advice given is to dress as if you had the next job up. This may not be possible in a company where most people wear the same kind of clothes, e.g. everyone wears navy suits. However, you can note what accessories the higher up people wear and buy them; for example, a particular kind of watch or ties or a smart briefcase.

27

More important with dress is to make sure that it is suitable for the occasion. If your company allows jeans during working hours that does not mean that you should turn up to inter-departmental meetings in jeans. Your image would take a downslide and your views would not be taken seriously. You may think it silly that people judge by dress but that is all most people have to go on when they first see you across the meeting table. Once you have won acceptance then you can put your ideas over.

There are courses in dress management, the 'dress for success' and 'colour' style courses. Opinions vary as to whether such courses are effective. Some people tell me that they produce an amazing transformation in people who attend them. Others say that such courses are ineffective and do not tell you anything you don't already know. The truth is that people who are truly confident of their own style probably do not need them, but most of us may be helped by a little guidance on the matter.

Such courses can be valuable if you have no idea at all about how to put a working wardrobe together. Otherwise look in the latest magazines or watch successful colleagues. Don't be afraid to ask your boss or colleagues for advice. Something along the lines of 'I've never been able to find a jacket that fits properly. I've always admired the fact that yours fits. Could you tell me where you got it?' If you don't ask, you'll never learn.

Buy good quality clothes with a lasting style and a few good accessories. It is a mistake to think that being well dressed means that you have to wear a complete new set of clothes every day. But you can ring the changes with ties, shirts and accessories (as long as they are not overdone), and everything kept clean and pressed. If you are working in a company which has a more informal atmosphere you can temper an informal general working style with putting on a jacket for meetings.

MODERATE YOUR IMAGE

Get into the habit of assessing each situation when you come into it. If you insist on either dressing in an informal or formal way all the time whatever the situation, your colleagues and clients will not empathise with you as much as they could. A simple method of changing your image to meet the situation is to take off your jacket. If you go into a meeting and everyone is relaxed and in shirtsleeves then do not cling to your jacket. Take it off and immediately you have become part of the group.

Similarly, if you need to appear more formal put a jacket on. This is particularly useful for women who, unlike men, do not always spend their whole time at work in a jacket. If they keep one handy then they can acquire a formal look immediately. Likewise men always appear formal wearing a jacket.

Manners maketh marketing

If you always act towards people in the same way, you will not always be doing your personal image a favour. For example, if you have a cheery brash image all the time this may go down well with some of your colleagues but grate on your superiors or clients. Equally, somebody who is generally quiet will not win marks if they fail to make an important point at a meeting and let colleagues down.

Good manners begins with considering the needs of others and making it easy for them to conduct whatever business is on hand. You should therefore adapt your personal style to different groups of people and individuals in order to put them at their ease and give them a chance to accept you. If that means moderating your behaviour, so be it. It is better to adapt than to lose a client or fail to get promotion. In any case, if you cannot make the effort to get on with people you will have a hard time progressing in any work situation. It should go without saying that the basic everyday manners of 'please' and 'thank you' and 'excuse me' should not be abandoned simply because you are at work. Simple courtesies show an awareness of your colleagues as human beings and individuals and make work an nicer place to be. Good manners towards everybody, including clients and the general public, are vital. Your image could suffer a severe blow very quickly if people perceived you to be generally rude or only polite in certain situations.

Jekyll and Hyde

You may think from reading this that you will need to make a complete change in your character to the extent of being almost unrecognisable. This is not the case. All you need to do is to make slight adjustments. If you try to change yourself completely it will not last for long and will strike a jarring note with other people.

You can tone down your jokes if you tend to make too many and those are too smutty. You can prepare a few words to say at a meeting if you are normally quiet. You can make an effort to give everyone a friendly greeting if you usually sidle by trying to ignore them. You can tidy up your clothes and hair or wear a different shirt and shoes.

You should not go in for a major transformation but aim to give out enough of the right signals to other people so that they find you acceptable and have confidence in you and your work.

TACTICS THAT WORK

- walk tall and sit up straight. Apart from saving you from backache this will make you appear taller and more in command
- be friendly but not effusive. A friendly smile and greeting go a long way
- prepare what you want to say
- be tidy and clean in your clothing and personal hygiene
- complete your work efficiently, on time and with enthusiasm
- don't be afraid to ask for help or to give it
- learn more about your subject

Weaknesses or warnings?

You may have decided that you don't fit in with your colleagues, company or clients or that you do not present an acceptable image to the general public. Now is the time to sit down and try to pinpoint the weaknesses in your image. This can be done by working out what you want your image to achieve and where you feel it falls down at present. Do you think you:

- lack presentation skills?
- are too shy or effusive?
- lack report writing skills?
- haven't a clue about how to dress properly?
- tend to gabble when making a report?
- find it difficult to communicate with clients?

How can you improve on your weaknesses and change them to work for your image? Let's use the above list as an example:

1. You lack presentation skills. These can be learnt at courses either in company time or outside work. You can practise such skills at home with your family and friends or in front of a mirror.

2. You are too shy or effusive. This requires some thought on your part. If you are too shy, make a point of saying one thing to each person you meet during the day. Even a simple 'Hello. Nice day, isn't it?' will suffice. It may not make you into the world's best conversationalist overnight but it will help you to get used to the sound of your own voice. You can write down points that you have to make at meetings. If you are over-effusive then you need to tone your voice down. Count to ten in your head before you speak and then only say a few words.

3. You lack reporting skills. These can be learnt with practice. The first and most difficult step, as with any of the weaknesses you may think you have, is to accept that it is a weakness and to seek help for it. Joining a group to learn how to write effectively will not only improve your report writing skills but will also help you in other areas of your work.

4. You haven't a clue how to dress properly. Most of us are a bit unsure. We read magazines, ask our friends and colleagues, copy people we admire at work or on TV. Courses are available too.

31

5. You tend to gabble when making a report. Write down what you want to say in full and then consciously read it at half what you think is your normal speed. Take a deep breath before you start, to calm yourself down, and pause at the end of each sentence – just slightly, to slow yourself down. Gabbling can be cured if you practise. Sit at home with a tape-recorder, read a passage from a book and play it back over again until you have trained yourself to speak at a reasonable speed. The tape-recorder trick is useful for any nervousness about speech.

6. You find it difficult to get on with clients. To get on with people you have to like them and this means starting with something in common. Make sure you are dressed appropriately for the occasion so that you feel at ease yourself. Then look for something in the other person you can relate to. It may only be the fact that you both buy your shirts from M & S. Releasing this will give you confidence that you are dealing with someone on your own wavelength. Make sure you have prepared what points you want to make. You will get on with people better if you know what you want to say and say it clearly. A smile and a friendly manner help, too.

How not to be seen through

If you change your image you will wonder if people will see through you to the person you were. No, not unless you are trying to change your image out of all recognition with your character. You might be able to change your image entirely from your normal self to last for a few months but then the strain would tell. Little things would give you away. The fact that only some of your reports were well prepared, a flamboyant neckerchief tied in a neat classic knot, a friendly smile which never reaches the eyes.

32

If, however, you base your image on the real you, then what people will see will be an extension of your basic personality and an improved and enhanced version of yourself. They will not think it out of place although they will notice the improvement. So do not be afraid of making the image alterations that you need.

What the professionals say

Jane Ageros. *Communications Manager in the Corporate Affairs Department of Abbey National plc*

I'm communications manager, which means that a large part of my job is that I am in charge of communications to our staff. My unit produces not only the monthly video but also arranges newsletters for staff. Through those I guess the culture is influenced quite heavily. What we try and do in the newsletters is to motivate people and create this feeling that they're stakeholders and that they are involved in the business, and therefore should amass as much knowledge about the business as they can.

What Abbey National wants to project is a very friendly, warm image. We're certainly perceived as more caring and more trustworthy than other organisations. Our staff are very warm and friendly and don't blind people with science. I think if you walk into any branch you can see that, and this is how our branches are perceived. Because in the end Abbey National is its branches to most people or it's the person they deal with when they 'phone our direct line services. How I treat my staff and how they react to me is important to what kind of product they produce for the rest of the staff. I try to give values to my staff probably most by modelling them, leading by example. Those values, which I then hope will go into staff newsletters, are such things as honesty and dealing with issues head on but in a positive way. I think that's very important. I think a negative culture or a whingeing culture can be counter-productive so I try and look at it from the positive point of view but also be honest, so it's not propaganda but it's not whingeing.

That's probably very much as a product of my personality. I like enthusiasm, I like energy and I hope that I can show to my staff that that's what I expect back. What I try to do with staff communications and indeed with my own staff, is to make them feel more like stakeholders in the business rather than just nine to fivers, make them see they can actually contribute to results, to the bottom line, to make Abbey National a success. And if Abbey National's a success then that's good for them because they work here. A lot of the staff are shareholders, a lot of staff get profit share. We can actually have a financial say in it but we can also use our energy and enthusiasm and dedication to drive the business forward.

I couldn't *not* be myself, I carry on as usual. But I wouldn't say certain things when I'm acting as representative of the company. I wouldn't, for instance, get involved in debates about a competitor or slag them off. I would be conscious of the fact that I'm for Abbey National, and I've got to present a positive front. I'm not there to be just another piece of propaganda, I'm still me. But I am committed to the company and I'm committed to telling other people outside the company that it's a good company, which I believe.

You do assume a professional persona. You do have to make a bit of an effort but it's got to be part of you otherwise you're just putting it on and it will show. It's interesting how companies do assume their own persona, do tend to attract people of that same persona to them. I think Abbey National is an open, friendly, forward-looking organisation. It's not stuffy and old-fashioned and therefore you attract that kind of person to you.

I know that from one branch to another the way staff people conduct mortgage interviews can vary terrifically. There are certain things they have to do because of legal acts and compliance issues, but personality isn't something we just sit on. I think you've got to adapt your personality for your customer but I think we allow flexibility within the Abbey National. Behaviour is less about being set down and more about just being in the system almost, in the air that you breathe. You watch the way your colleagues act and you pick that up. There'll be some things, such as you must be polite to the customers, you must be friendly. The more difficult stuff to pick up you just imbibe, almost by being in Abbey National, you see how people react. You have to do what comes naturally but you'll have your manager to coach you in whether or not what you're doing is working, is appealing to customers. We have training on customer skills, or training on different aspects of management, or training on communications skills for managers, but not actually on image. But again I think a lot of image is almost picked up through values which have been around for a long time which people just know about instinctively and which are reinforced through staff communications.

I wouldn't say I reassess my image because that's almost too Machiavellian, as if you're trying to be something you're not. I do think about it. As a woman manager you have to think about it with a with a female angle as well and I've been on assertiveness training and found that very helpful. I'm actually quite an honest person and so occasionally I think 'well, I should stop saying what I mean so much', that kind of tinkering.

I think also as a manager you have to assess how you're relating to your staff. Sometimes you may feel you want to get closer to a particular member of staff. Sometimes perhaps you've got too friendly and you need to back off a bit in order to be objective. So there are minor tinkerings but I don't have a kind of image plan. I don't really buy into that stuff of creating image, you've got to be you. It's just you've got to be the professional side of you, not the home side of you.

Apart from the assertiveness course I've been on presentation courses. But it's more like a tool of your image, it's not image itself. It's more a skill that you learn. I was offered a chance to go on one of these colour courses but I feel that I should know what colour makes me feel good and makes me look good. I'm always a bit cynical about that.

We do have an appraisal system half-yearly and yearly, and part of it is that you ask your staff what *you* could be doing better. I think one measure of whether you do get on is how honest they are at that stage and I find that my staff do say things. Sometimes that can just be a lip service contribution but staff do contribute; my staff do seem to tell me when there's a problem, when they don't agree with something I say and I think that's a pretty good measure of whether you're operating well as a manager. I think dictatorial managerial styles are pretty much out nowadays. If you're not getting the best ideas out of people then you're narrowing the bets because you're only getting ideas out of one person and the manager. I think the atmosphere in my team is friendly and warm and there are no great crises. We pull together when hard work is needed.

A couple of my staff have not been assertive enough in the past and I've said 'look, if you're going to get the best out of your job, you're going to have to start being a bit more proactive and speaking more at meetings and influencing more and networking', but that's more a kind of internal image, though in the end it does affect customers because that's their job. I think probably the way I've presented myself has a great deal to do with the way I've progressed in the company, because I've presented myself as someone who's hardworking, dedicated to getting results, a lot of common sense; I'm not going to start infighting; I've got my eye very much on the means of the business; I'm positive, not taking myself too seriously, and I think being honest, too. I think in that way you can get on because they like people who are based on results, they like people who are positive, they like people who are not afraid to speak their mind whilst at the same time having tact. You don't want someone who makes a virtue out of speaking their mind

35

because that's as bad as the opposite. Any manager wants to recruit staff with enthusiasm and energy. That's what my manager wants and I guess I've showed that and managers have seen I've got that and promoted me. There's nothing worse than a member of staff who isn't really there in spirit and can't get the results out at all.

Internally we're very big on a new quality programme and I think that you do reassess your behaviour in the light of things to do with the quality. Like 'am I always based on results? Do I always act quickly enough? Do I give internal customer service?', that kind of thing.

I think you do have to accept that when you work at Abbey National, wherever you go you are a person who's telling the customer something about Abbey National. I don't think that should affect your behaviour when you're with friends or in private, but if Abbey National comes up you do project a positive image about it. There are certain things that as a member of staff you wouldn't do but then I wouldn't do them as a person, anyway. You have to be somewhat aware, especially as you get more senior, that what you say about Abbey National will be taken as representing the company view and you have to be aware of that. Putting out some company line or lying would be silly but you have to stress the benefits and be positive rather than whinge and be negative.

I've never said anything to my staff about dress and they've just quite naturally adopted different dress because we're in head office and not in constant contact with the customer. Some of my staff wear very casual trousers to work. It's quite a free and easy department in a way. Personally I do tend to wear women's suits, a skirt and jacket and maybe a splash of colour on the top. At the weekend I'll go round seriously casual, and I feel different so I act more casual.

I can think of occasions where if you have a particular suit you feel confident in then you would wear it at an important meeting, say yellow, or not too bright but just quite smart, very tailored and very professional. And wearing heels actually helps me because I'm not that tall. I think if my staff are in for an ordinary day and they've got no meetings then they wear what they like and I react to them just as a person. But in a meeting I think probably they would dress up more smartly and I would react to them differently.

I think that for women in general management it's quite difficult for women working in a masculine dominated world to present the right image. Some women go too far and say 'I'll be like a stereotypical man', i.e. macho, aggressive, dynamic kind of style. Sometimes it doesn't come naturally to women but they feel that's how you have to act. But I think in the end if you're not being yourself you're going to come a cropper. Also I think that as a woman you have to sometimes slightly redress the balance with your assertiveness, because there is a sense in which women have been conditioned to behave in a less assertive manner than men which sometimes doesn't work at a meeting. On the other hand you shouldn't go too far in the other direction. I think it is quite difficult for women to get that balance right, but if you need results, not just in the business but in your own career, then I think you do have to pay a certain amount of attention to how you are perceived in predominantly male management.

There are so many more men than women managers that I do think men are different towards their superiors. I've only got one male member of staff. He's a lot younger so it's probably not representative because he's the most junior member of the department, anyway. But because he's younger it's easier. Possibly if he was older than me that would be different but in general I try not to react differently to men. Although I think sometimes you have to adapt yourself to different styles of communication, with them and what's expected of both sexes you have to take into account and carry forward.

LEARNING POINTS CHECKLIST

1 See how you fit into the management image

2 Assess your company's management image

3 Decide what style you want to develop

4 Adapt your image to your own personality

5 Dress to impress

6 Adapt your image to the situation

7 Don't forget basic good manners

8 Discover your weaknesses and change them

9 Don't be afraid of making changes to your image

10 Adopt a friendly manner

DAY TWO ACTION PLAN

In the previous chapter you assessed your image and what you wanted to do to change it. Now you must assess the management image and see how your own image fits into that. Write down what you want to achieve in your work. Make two lists, one of long-term, the other of short-term, aims. See if there is any common denominator in the list, e.g. need for report writing skills or presentation skills.

Now make a list of your characteristics and temperament and something about your present image. See how it fits into the previous list. What needs changing? How can you do it? Don't forget to include information about dress, your own, that of the company, that of people you admire. How can you adapt your present dress style?

If you think you need particular training make a note of it and see what your company, local classes, distance learning, books and magazines have to offer. Nowadays there are also management videos to help you. Commit yourself to one learning method.

Make a list of your weaknesses and write down two ways you can improve on each of them. Tomorrow make a start by giving a friendly greeting and a smile to everyone you meet. Make sure you have a tape-recorder at home so that you can practise your speaking skills. Practise a bit every day.

4

Your work image

Your clients and the public at large are not the only people you need to sell yourself to. Your personal image can affect how your colleagues, staff and boss react to you and how your work is valued within the company.

It is possible to be excellent at your job and to work very hard and yet still feel that your work is undervalued and unappreciated within your own company. Do not forget that however good you are at your work people will not appreciate it unless you can ensure that its value is brought to their attention in a way that they can understand. It also needs to be presented to them by somebody (you) whom they can relate to.

If you are the quiet type who mumbles whenever asked to present a paper then your work may be good but nobody will know it. Or if you turn up to a meeting with your boss without the relevant papers you will be regarded as inefficient, however brilliant your research. To improve your image at work you have to determine how your colleagues perceive you and to decide which group in the company you are trying to impress. Is it the boss or your staff? Is it the head of department or the tea person? Once you recognise how others see you and you have worked out where you want to go in the company, then you can plan your career strategy and how to alter your image to boost your progress.

This chapter will help you find out how others in your work place see you, how to decide which group of people at work to impress and how to alter your image to give the right message to each group. It will also show you how to capitalise on your strengths, discover what opportunities are coming up, and gear your image to make the maximum gains.

You will also have day three of your ten-day image plan to help you on your way.

Who loves you, baby?

Apart from eavesdropping when your colleagues are talking about you or tapping your boss's phone, how can you find out how people at work perceive you?

This is not easy. Most people never do discover exactly what people at work think of them. They go on in blissful ignorance and either assume that they are, on the whole, liked, or become gloomy and adopt an 'everyone is against me' resentful attitude to the world at large.

Nowadays many large organisations provide training courses. Some of these may provide a 'let's be honest with each other' feedback situation. If your company offers this type of course then do take it. Even if you don't like what is said it will still valuable feedback. Or perhaps your departmental head encourages honesty in the monthly team meeting – 'air your grievances'. This too can be useful.

You could be straightforward and ask: 'John, I need some ideas on how I'm handling this presentation. I'd really appreciate it if you'd give me some honest feedback on how I put myself over'. Either the recipient of this request will back off in horror and embarrassment or will give you a scathingly honest run down of your defects. It's worth a try. You can judge quite a lot by interpretation of people's reactions to you. But be careful. You may interpret the fact that nobody has been to your office for three days as a personal slight, whereas they may all have their heads down trying to finish an urgent report. If, however, every time you give a report to a group of people you find that halfway through people start talking, or when you are in a meeting your contributions are constantly dismissed, then clearly you are doing something wrong.

HOW DO THEY SEE YOU?

Make a list of how you think your colleagues, staff, boss, the

40

cook and anyone else at work sees you. Be honest, but also include positive points. If you are entirely negative you will only depress yourself and this will cause inaction.

Which group to impress?

You may be thinking, 'If I impress the boss, I'm made' and be tempted to ignore other groups of people at work. Of course you want your boss to think favourably of you but you do not want to be undermined by colleagues. If your boss is inclined to look favourably on you but you have antagonised several of your colleagues you can be sure that it will get back to your boss. Even if what is said or hinted is unfounded, the fact that there is unpleasantness at all will count against you. Office politics cannot be ignored. If you make enemies in the office and rely only on your skill at work to see you through, you are doomed to failure.

41

So you must present a favourable image to your colleagues and your staff. You don't want them going over your head to complain about you. You want a hard-working, enthusiastic team who clearly support you. If you don't have that your managerial skills will be in doubt. Don't ignore the other staff, the tea person, the canteen staff, reception, security, secretaries, and so on. If you are offhand or unpleasant to them they can not only make life unpleasant for you but will make sure word gets back to somebody who will use it to undermine you.

WHICH IS THE MOST IMPORTANT GROUP?

This is a trick question. Hands up everyone who said 'the boss'? No points. A gold star to everyone who said 'everyone'! You cannot afford to ignore anyone in the office situation. That is not to say that there will not be different ways of presenting yourself to different groups in the office. But your image should be acceptable to everyone from the boss to the cleaner.

What will it cost me?

Adapting your image may cost you something, but how much will depend on what aspects of your image you are trying to change. Changing your way of speaking, your personality, or your attitude to work will cost you nothing except time and trouble. Changing your clothes or hairstyle or updating your skills may cost you money – possibly a great deal. Much will depend on how much investment and time you can put into your image. I hope I can persuade you that it is worth the effort and some financial outlay.

CLOTHES

You can spend a few pounds on a new tie or pocket hanky or a hundred pounds on a watch. A suit can cost less than two hundred pounds or hundreds more. Remember that if you buy something cheap and only wear it once it costs more in terms of cost per wearing than if you buy something expensive about wear it often.

Go for quality. Keep up to date with style but don't make it excessive. Keep your clothing appropriate to your job. There is a saying 'dress for the job above' so that you look as if you are promotable to the next rung up. One or two good sets of clothes kept clean and mended although worn frequently are better than lots of cheap clothes. If you can afford to go on a 'style' or 'colour' course it may give you some ideas even if you don't agree entirely with what they say. But you can save money by reading about fashion in books and magazines.

TRAINING

Here again the cost can vary. It could be an MBA or an adult education class, an Open University course or a book from the library.

If you tell me you don't need any more training then I wonder what is wrong with you. Unless you keep up to date with your skills and expertise, and look into a specialist section of your work, then you will not make a good impression. Somebody who is out of date and still quoting theory and practice from 10 years ago is not the stuff of which high fliers are made. Training also keeps your brain turning and ideas flowing. You may not agree with the latest thoughts on your subject but you must know enough about them to be able to argue a different point of view. You may not need a full-blown MBA. If your company does like its senior managers to have it then it may pay for training whether full or part-time. You can also study it at home with the Open University. If your firm won't pay then it should be well within the scope of your personal finances.

If your job requires professional skills and information then it is clearly important to make sure that you update these regularly. Your image will suffer if people see you as out of date. It is particularly important to keep up to date in areas where new knowledge, for example of the law or tax rules, makes a great deal of difference to what you should be telling your clients or advising your colleagues. Consider other areas of training. What about courses on presentation skills, assertiveness, motivation, report writing, staff management, finance, economics? If your organisation doesn't provide these then you may find them at adult education classes.

It is also advisable to develop expertise in one section of your work as well as having a broad skill base. An expert is always in demand. This can be done either by home-based study or extra-mural classes, or even by reading round the subject in books and periodicals.

Do not begrudge money spent on training. It may seem a large part of your time and finances to commit to learning but it is constructive and useful. If you really want to improve your image at work then you must have the right knowledge background and you must look upon it as an investment in your future.

PERSONAL ATTRIBUTES

It is perfectly possible to alter your personality and personal attributes by simply practising in front of a mirror or by asking your partner to correct you whenever you do something unacceptable. This is free, though time-consuming, but can be done with perseverance. However, there are courses in personal development. Assertiveness training is one obvious example. There is no doubt that such courses where you can practise techniques with other people will help you progress more quickly. If the company does not organise these, ask at your library for adult education classes.

REFERENCE MATERIAL

You must keep up to date with your area of expertise at work. If you are in one of the professions or trades then there will undoubtedly be a periodical geared to that subject. Your in-house journal is a useful source of information about what the company provides and what information is available. Many of the 'heavier' magazines and newspapers contain articles which are pertinent to your work. Radio and television programmes are useful (watch the Open University programmes even if you don't do the courses). Reference books on your subject can be obtained from bookshops and libraries. Even videos have their place.

44

You do not necessarily need to have a personal copy of every up-to-date book, article or video on your subject but you should read a lot about it and the related business scene. I do insist that it is vital to read one broadsheet newspaper every day and one Sunday heavyweight paper if you are to keep up adequately with the world.

Which message for which group?

At the end of the day you can only be you. You will have your own base core of personality to present to the world. But you will need to adapt that to different groups of people at work. For example, if you have to present a paper to the sales department you will draw on your experiences and knowledge of sales to put your thoughts over in a way which they would appreciate and can relate to. People relate best to what seems familiar and seems to fit in with them. If you insist on turning up to speak at a conference as the bumbling scientist you are, with three red biros in your jacket pocket and your shirt hanging out, your great thoughts will be lost on an audience who cannot hear you and even if they can will not be inclined to listen to someone who does not strike them as presenting an sympathetic image.

How to boost your career progression

To get ahead in your career you need to spot what the trends are in your company and adapt your personal image to make the most of them in a timely way.

Keep an eye on what sort of people seem to be getting ahead. Last year it was straitlaced accountants because the company was in an economic trough. At the moment it is wild-eyed creative types because the company is now on a firmer footing and needs some bright ideas to keep it there. You notice that training is being given at the moment to good team leaders with presentation experience. Now is the time to improve your presentation skills, at your own expense if necessary, and to take a more active part in team work if you haven't before. Try to look ahead as far as expertise is concerned. You can see that desktop publishing is the next move for the sales department because they are looking for ways to get their material out more quickly. Now is the time to become the department expert on desktop publishing. Train, learn, gently make it known that you know your subject and when the department finally make the decision to go ahead, you will be the person they think of.

What your boss needs

If you want to develop your image in a way which will impress your boss then you have to know what he or she is looking for. It is no good being quiet and good at economics if your boss has decided to develop the creative side of the business and is looking for confident ideas people.

Keep a sharp look out for trends within the organisation. If there seem to be more people being promoted on the creative

45

side or the technology side it will be worth your while seeing what skills you have in that direction and extending them. If technology is the new thing and you know about finance why not take some training in spreadsheet and financial management using computers? You will then be ideally placed to take on the new technology with your new and old skills combined.

It is rarely the case that people can tackle a completely new skill in enough depth and in time to make a complete changeover at short notice. So it makes sense to identify an area of need and adapt one of your existing strengths to it. If your boss tends towards using more brash creative people you could take an assertiveness course together with a desktop publishing course. It won't turn you into a confident designer overnight but you will start to hold your own in that sort of company and have a relevant skill to offer. As a manager, courses in financial management or presentation can be combined with other strengths to turn you into the sort of person your seniors are watching out for.

How to spot the spaces

It is not always the case that vacancies will be made known within the organisation in good enough time for you to prepare for them. If you are thinking of looking outside your own organisation it is even more difficult to find out what is going on. Often advertised vacancies, whether inside or outside the company, are already spoken for and the interviews are a formality. You need to find ways of keeping in front.

Use friends and acquaintances ruthlessly. Tell people that you are on the lookout for something suitable and listen carefully when the subject of jobs comes up. You need to project an image to seniors of someone ready to take on a new job at any moment, and do this at the same time as finding out where the vacancies occur, so you can apply for them. Make sure that you are looking your best and are getting work done with enthusiasm and on time. If you are taking relevant courses you can let it be known in the course of conversation so that other people are aware that you have or are obtaining relevant skills or information. Keep in the office eye by attending functions in and out of work time. Volunteer for occasions such as conferences where you can practise and demonstrate your newly acquired training.

All these things will keep you in people's minds while you are working towards that new post. Your image will be one of someone who is ready to step into the job.

HAVE YOU MADE IT?

You won't know that you have finally made it until you have taken the next step up the ladder or won the plum post you were angling for. However, you can get an idea of how you are doing by whether your opinion is sought by your seniors more often, whether colleagues say 'I heard my boss mention your name to the chief executive today', and whether your boss starts making casual enquiries about your aims.

If you want to get on your image does have to project confidence, even quietly, and the ability to communicate with others. It cannot be said too often that backroom brilliance will get you nowhere if your image doesn't fit what the clients, or your superiors, want to see. You must get yourself and your ideas out into the market-place in a suitable form and be able to let others know the quality of your work and yourself.

Public relations officer

Public relations officers in any organisation have a specialised job. It is their duty to make sure that the organisation is presented in the best possible light. They have to publicise the company and deflect bad publicity. It is worth taking a tip out of their books. If something good happens they let the world know. If something bad happens they get their version in first and try to minimise the damage. Your PRO can help you improve your image.

If you have done something worthwhile, maybe outside work, such as winning a sporting trophy or publishing a book, then let your company know it. Do not hide your light under a bushel, or

47

anything else. How can you expect people to take your good points into account if you don't tell people they are there? When things go wrong do not try to pretend that they haven't. Admit your mistake and ask for help straightaway. Learn why you went wrong and take steps to correct it. If you ruined a presentation because you ran out of steam in the middle then you must ask for training in presentation skills and learn how to prepare enough clear notes to see you through any presentation.

It is worth your while getting to know your public relations officer. You may not think that you will have much to do with public relations but more and more companies are using people from within their own organisation rather than professional actors to appear in company videos or on television advertisements. If you are known to them, willing, and your image fits the image the company wants the world to see, then you have a good chance of being used when such a situation comes up.

48

People from outside the company often want to talk to representatives of the company (for example, for this book I asked the PR departments of major companies to find me someone to talk to about image). If you are considered someone who will make interesting interviewing material and will represent the company in a good light then you will be called upon. If you make yourself known to the PRO as an expert on a particular aspect of the company then you can be called on as the company expert in that area – even if the area is quite small and specialised.

Once you have got to know your PRO and have represented the company in some kind of media event your image will undergo a subtle change in the eyes of other people. To the general public you will be to some extent the company because it is you whose opinion and/or face they will have seen. By your colleagues you will be viewed with a mixture of envy and respect. Many will claim that *they* wouldn't have wanted to do it but will envy the fact that it was *you* who were asked. Your opinion obviously counts for something. If you handle the media situation well your bosses will mentally mark you down as someone who can be trusted to represent the company without being stuffy and who has a body of knowledge which is an asset to them.

TRAINING FOR THE MEDIA

The subject of facing the media is tackled in greater detail in Chapter Eight. Suffice it to say here that if you want to be of use to the PRO as an individual who can represent the company, but you feel you lack the necessary skills, do not let this deter you from offering your services. Just make sure that you put the problem to the PRO and take their advice. If they suggest further training take it.

Individuals

Not everyone will want to present the same image at work. If you are on the creative side you may wish to appear more in tune with your colleagues' image of flamboyance and brashness than with the accountants with their sober suits and serious conversations. But do not generalise too much. It is possible to be creative in manner but still present yourself in a jacket and tie and make a clear, sensible presentation to your colleagues in other sections of the company. If you are an accountant you are allowed to smile!

You can bow to people's expectations to a certain extent. It will obviously be easier to work with your colleagues if your image does not stray too wildly from theirs. People are happier with similar people because they find them easier to relate to, but that does not mean you need to drown your natural personality entirely or not adapt it to other situations.

What the professionals say

Hilary Perkins. *Business Development Director for a major manufacturing company*

My job has very recently changed. I retain profit responsibility for my old department. But now I've been given the brief to go off and find new business opportunities within the professional market.

This company is very keen to change its image. If you ask

49

most people what the image of this company actually is they will think of little old ladies knitting in corners and doing typing. Actually we now provide material for quite an upscale market. So we really need to change our image and try to create the feeling that people are somewhat different. The route we've taken in my department has been to do some very nifty kind of brand associations which then mean that this company's image has a secondary importance, frankly, in terms of the buyer's perception. Nevertheless, we get pulled up by that image. Now people do see us as a dynamic company.

As an individual, I have a general view about what professionalism is and it's to do with excellence and with providing good service in whatever context. I think I also push the limits in terms of how open I am within that professionalism. With my staff I think I'm quite easy to approach – maybe I'm never in my office, but I'm actually quite approachable. Likewise I don't adopt a very formal way with other people, either customers or clients. I think I'm very consistent, in that always I tend to give the impression that there's the possibility of laughter and amusement there but there's a very hard core of professionalism underneath and nobody's going to be able to take me for a ride professionally. But then equally they can trust me because I pride myself on the quality of the work I do. I think that on the whole I don't have a very awkward way of approaching how to behave professionally.

Our company doesn't lay down any rules about image in general or what style individuals should adopt. I think we want every intersection we have with the outside world to give the impression that we're professional and we do a good job and we do a good job fast. We certainly don't define how people should behave, what they should say, what their modus operandi should be.

You ask me if I project a particular image myself. I think the image that I project is that my colleagues and I are undivided. As far as I'm concerned I can change ideas, I can come up with new ideas and look at the things in a fresh way now. The more interesting thing about that is that it's possibly to do with my role within the organisation, in that I'm pretty much seen as the company entrepreneur and maybe in a different culture and a different organisation I would come across in a very different way. We joke about it in the management team that it's important for me not to be seen as the resident creative, but I think I am!

My colleagues are used to me looking at things from a different angle and being the one in a meeting to say 'hey, hang on a minute, have you thought about it this way?'. We were doing a strategic review of the company and I was very involved in co-ordinating it with the managing director. I think everybody was slightly surprised that he'd chosen me to do that with him because I'm not viewed as a finisher. In fact, I am terribly dogged once it gets to getting to complete a task.

But I think it's interesting how in a particular team you take on a role and you develop that role and sometimes it can be to the detriment of other aspects of your working personality. Now I've moved into a job where that side of me is obviously going to be very predominant. If I'd moved into a job where I had far more people to manage or something like that I don't know whether that would have been the case.

51

I don't make a conscious effort to change my image. If a colleague said something, I'd probably take it on board and try and act on it. But the thing that really triggers me to change my behaviour is to see policies not working and to realise that I'm part of that failure.

There have been working relationships which have not been particularly easy and where I've sat back and I've thought 'okay, so what's the way to deal with this?' and it's not always the case that I'm really successful at making it into a better relationship. But at least I put some effort into trying to change it. In particular I've done that with the people who work for me, because I think for them it's very much more difficult to have somebody who is so unclear as to what's she's going to say next, what idea's going to come up next. Actually I think most people respond to quite a structured working environment. Maybe I'm wrong, but I think that risk-taking is something that is a relatively rare. Whether I'd risk-take with my own money, I don't know!

As far as managers' personal image is concerned I think the way they present themselves definitely affects how the public sees the company. I think some companies really do suggest a way of behaviour to their staff and I don't think this company does. But I think that in a publishing relationship the kind of charismatic power or lack of it, the interaction with the outside world, is one of the most powerful things. Our business is made up of unconventional contractual arrangements because there are so many external things playing on both parties. Our clients have got to really like what they see in the person they deal with, I think, and feel that this is somebody who's going to enrich their lives – somebody they want to spend time with.

I think a consistent enthusiasm and kind of upbeat approach to the general public helps reinforce what we're trying to achieve here, so that whenever anybody meets somebody from this company they capture an enthusiasm for what's going on in the company. This will have a big impact on changing our image and making our company more successful.

Do my colleagues take my advice about how they present themselves? They do listen, although I can never really tell because I'm not there when they go back and talk to the others. I certainly listen to them. For example, my boss will quite often say things about written presentation or verbal presentation. He will give me advice about how he would handle the situation and we're very different personalities. I think we admire different things in one another and that's very fruitful. He may say to me, 'well, how about handling it this way?' and I probably hadn't thought of it because we're temperamentally quite different.

The question about whether my personal image has helped me progress through the company is a tricky one. I think I come as a package and so far I've been fortunate in being quite successful with the various things I've done. I think I have quite a forceful personality and I have to be aware when it's not always having the right effect. Coupled with that I'm good at what I do. I don't think there are many jobs where you can be absolutely outstanding on the presentation side and not make the 'phone call the next day and not actually add up the numbers you need correctly. I think it is the package that counts. But I don't think an individual who had all the kind of implementation skills that I have but none of the, frankly, self-promotion, would go as far.

I'm somebody who's quite brave. I revel in showing my head above the parapet – but that's quite a risky business because the falls and the downside are really pretty tough. You've laid so much on the line that it's your personality that's at risk if your career begins to falter. But that is very much the approach I've adopted and I think it's been quite important to my success. But it's not that any one bit of that mix of personality and competence is less or more important than anything else.

I do think there are some areas of my image that need working on. For example, this issue of openness, it's not that I necessarily need to change it, but I think as you get up in other organisations people probably expect you to become more dis-tant and less easily read and that's going to be difficult for me. I'm not very like that, although actually there's a lot about me that people don't know in the work environment. But I think I create the impression of being very much all there 'in your face' as they say in America, and I'm not sure about that 'in your faceness'. Maybe it's going to be something I'm going to have to modify as I grow older and get more senior.

I'm quite inexperienced in encountering people who have problems with the way I am and so I think I'm still learning a lot about that. When I encounter clients who are very contained and have very different personalities and style, then I think I just become more distant in approach myself. But I think on the colleague level I've got a lot to learn about the downside of the way I am. I think the upside is probably that I can be quite motivational and inspiring to the people around me but the downside is that they can feel as if they're going to teeter along a precipice and they're not actually quite sure what they should be doing next because somebody's giving them such a long leash that they can't even shout for help. I think I need to learn how to cope with that and to be much more directive without clipping people's wings.

You've asked me whether courses are available. This com-pany is pretty good on training and courses are available. We all did a course on performance in the workplace which was rather an experiment. I think we all learnt a lot from that. I certainly learnt a lot about how I behave in the workplace.

53

There are problems about taking presentation courses with groups. Maybe one of the problems with the course we did was that for a really good presentation course you need somebody to just sit with the individual and work to maximise the effectiveness of what you're doing. I think I could benefit from somebody sitting with me and saying, 'this is you, this is the way you present yourself and you're going to encounter these kind of obstacles'. I don't know how you improve your presentation skills without having had personal help. Nobody sees my presentation as particularly a problem at the moment, but it might become a problem later.

I obviously don't engender a terribly corporate style in the department. I feel when we're all working here, particularly all summer when it's frankly far too hot, we should be relaxed so that we can work hard. My own practice when I'm meeting customers and business clients is to try and get some sense of what the dress code will be and I can go to anything from really corporate to almost the long floaty skirt and open-toed sandals. I feel that what you need to do is to dress to get results and I think if you turn up in a very corporate outfit in an environment that makes people feel uncomfortable you're going to have as bad an effect as if you go into a city bank wearing shorts. I think it's a question of being very sensitive and trying to find out what the dress code's going to be.

I suppose the point is that all of my clothes are in a spectrum. I don't possess anything that is probably as corporate as corporate dress but I do have some outfits where somebody corporate would look at it and say, this is someone from a non-corporate business making an effort. At the other end of the spectrum I have just non-corporate clothes. As far as adapting my image to different situations goes, I can be very consistent in the way I describe the company and what I say about it. But maybe if I'm meeting a client with an ad agency I'll dredge up my experience of people I know or experiences I've had in that world, and if I'm talking to somebody who's a communications trainer in Bradford or something like that I'll likewise find part of my experience that has some kind of intersection with theirs. So I think the fringes of your conversation undergo personality change but not the core.

I think it's very important for the individual to feel that there's a consistency between what the company wants to achieve and what they want to achieve. I think it's very important to communicate and reach a sense of agreement with what's going on in a company and have commitment to it, and that's very much a personal thing. I think when people meet me they probably get that impression. I'm not necessarily wowed by the content of my job but I'm certainly wowed by the process and by the opportunity and I think it's very important to communicate that impression to as many people as I can because otherwise you can't actually achieve what you need to achieve.

LEARNING POINTS CHECKLIST

1 Work out what others feel about you at work
2 Decide which groups at work you want to impress
3 Decide what image each group prefers
4 Decide what image improvement you need to spend money on
5 Capitalise on your strengths
6 Don't be modest about your achievements
7 Keep an eye on company trends
8 Make the most of opportunities
9 Get to know your PRO
10 Take the PRO's advice about meeting the media

DAY THREE ACTION PLAN

If your company provides training courses with feedback on individuals' management style, enrol for one. Do not be depressed by what is said. Make notes and use them as a starting point for image improvement. In your notebook write a list of all the different groups whom you will have to meet during the course of your work. Write down how you think they will expect to perceive you. Tick where you do fulfil those expectations and look at the points where you don't. Make a note to change to fit those expectations. List the groups in order of importance, if there is one. Ask yourself why you think some groups are more important that another.

Work out how much you can afford to spend on clothing and training.

55

Make a list of expenditure over the next six months. Write a list of clothes you will need and the cost of training or classes. Include the cost of useful management or image books you intend to buy as well as the cost of subscriptions to professional and trade magazines and journals. If your budget is tight look at your list and work out how you can cut this expenditure down, e.g. by visiting the library once a week or saving up for one classic piece of clothing.

Take steps to find out what your boss and company's future needs will be. Ask the personnel manager, your colleagues, secretaries. Make a list of these and work out how your expertise can fit in with these future expectations and how you will need to improve to take advantage of them. Find out who your public relations officer is and arrange to meet him or her. Ask about media training and whether there are any opportunities to take part in media events either as participant or observer.

56

5

Promoting yourself at work

As a commodity in the work market-place you are on show all the time. You need to sell yourself to your colleagues, staff, boss and any visitors to your work environment.

For most of the time you will be presenting yourself on a one-to-one basis with individuals within your organisation – when you speak to your secretary or chat to your colleague in the next office. But there are times when you will have to make sure your image is suitable for special occasions when you will be seen by many people.

Some of these situations are environmental ones – the company which believes in open-plan offices and/or glass panelled office suites, or eating in the staff canteen, for example. Others arise from the nature of the situation such as board meetings, interviewing staff or advising your seniors. This chapter tells you how to make sure that you present the best image possible in those situations and explains how to deal with the problems that arise.

One to one

Your most common image problem is with the individuals you deal with at work on a day-to-day basis. It is no good saying that because you are in a work situation you can forget your image. Image is not just for the outside world. You need to influence those people you work with and meet every day just as much as the occasional visitor, the general public or your customers. If you are slovenly about your image at work, it will affect how you do your work and how you treat it. It will also give an unfavourable impression to those at work who are in a position to help you progress. If you don't take your image seriously people will assume that you don't take your work seriously.

You should also bear in mind that although you may spend all your day in a work situation where you do not come into contact with the general public, there may be occasions, perhaps unexpected, when you do so. You shouldn't have to change your work image if the Queen comes to call – it should be presentable to everyone at all times.

FACE TO FACE

It is important that you treat people you come into contact with at work as individuals. It is not good enough to adopt an offhand manner with everyone except the boss. You will soon become disliked or at the best tolerated. Everyone is a person with their own views, aspirations, likes and dislikes. You should make the effort to respond to everyone as a person with a unique view to offer and worthy of individual consideration.

58

Image seesaw

Don't forget that there is no one route on which to project a personal image. You have to project it in many different directions. For your boss you have to project it up, for colleagues sideways and for your staff downwards. For the general public and clients you must project outwards, to yourself you project inwards.

If this sounds complicated it is only another way of saying that you must adapt your image to the situation and to the people involved. You would be unlikely to show your boss the same flippant attitude to your work that you might adopt with a friend, for example. If you did, you would not last long in your job!

For your boss you need to be respectful but not afraid of making your views clear. You need to be slightly more formal than usual and at the same time appear confident in yourself and your work. For your colleagues you need to be enthusiastic about work, helpful, friendly and able to indulge in small talk if the occasion demands it. For your staff you need to be approachable, reassuring, helpful, supportive and encouraging.

Again you do not need to alter your image drastically to do this. You might put your jacket on to see the boss and call her Mrs Brown rather than Mary. You might call your colleagues Joe and Sally and take your jacket off and make the occasional joke. For your staff you may call everyone by their first name but be slightly more formal when it comes to discussing work with them.

How you expect to be treated will vary, too. You may not expect your boss to call you Jill but you may wish your staff and colleagues to do so. You may allow your staff to dress informally at work but at the same time prefer them to put a jacket on and call you Mr Jones when talking to you in your office.

Decide how you expect people to behave to you at all levels, and work out how you should behave to them. Be careful not to deviate too much from group to group. If you change from very informal to over-formal frequently you will confuse and upset people, because they will not be able to work out how to react to you on any given occasion.

59

You need to decide how far you will socialise with different people out of work. You may want to socialise with the boss but it may not be possible! You may decide that some colleagues you like and others you only want to see at work. Then you will have to be careful about how you treat the people you see out of work when you are in the office. You have to be friendly but not show any favouritism. You have to be aware that you must treat their work and your relationship with them just as you do your other colleagues, otherwise there will be a lot of in-fighting.

As for your staff, fraternising with them has its advantages and dangers. It is perfectly acceptable to attend such things as Christmas dinners or staff concerts and parties if everyone else does. But if you spend too much time with one or two particular members of your staff you lay yourself open to charges of favouritism. You may find that to hold yourself a little distant from your staff means that they treat you with more respect than if you tried to join in everything they do. Having said that, many organisations provide amenities which are enjoyed by all ranks of staff alike. Sports centres, choirs, health clubs and so on. Of course it is sensible to use these facilities if they are available and you can be friendly to anyone from work who also uses them, without compromising your position.

For each group you should work out how formal or informal you will be in terms of:

- dress
- names
- greetings
- socialising
- instruction

The persuasive image

A fair estimate would be that about 50% of your job is image. It is not an extra which is just the concern of the company or the PR managers. Very few people are swayed by the pure logic of an argument. They want to like the person who is presenting the argument and to find the way it is said acceptable. It is no good being a manger unless you can persuade other people such as your boss, colleagues, suppliers and clients to agree to things. You need to get people to change their point of view and get them to argue so that you can counter their objections. It is not just what you say that will convince people to change their minds, it is how you say it. So you need to adapt your style of speaking to the occasion.

But you need to present an image which is acceptable to your audience. For example, a bank manager is not likely to be persuaded to finance a new idea by someone wearing a dirty T-shirt, scruffy jeans and who mumbles. This may seem unfair but it is only human nature to prefer that which is familiar and therefore seems reliable. You need to use several important persuasive tactics to get your own way:

1. Establish points of contact, not differences. Practically anything that makes people feel akin to you in some way will help. This is why it is important to note any personal details of people you deal with that you can use to form a bond. Maybe you both have young children or both play golf? Mentioning that at the beginning of a meeting can ease the situation. In the same way, if you are going to speak to someone who is dressed informally you could remove your jacket even if you arrive formally dressed. This kind of gesture makes you a part of the situation and you are not stressing your differences by remaining completely formal.

2. Stress the positive rather than the negative things. You may have in common that you both hate the staff canteen. But this gives any meeting a negative stance. Better to stress that you both like something. Consider this example. Two senior managers met. They were on rather bad terms and the initiator of the meeting was worried about how to ease the situation.

He discovered that the other manager smoked and was angry about the new non-smoking policy in the staff canteen. Rather than agree and stress the negative side of the situation, the first manager broke his own non-smoking rule and accepted a cigarette from his colleague. Without a word being said he had stressed the positive thought that he had smoking in common with the other manager and that he sympathised with him about the canteen. Nobody would advocate a return to smoking but the principle remains. Stress the positive things you have in common.

61

3. If there are differences which everyone recognises then mention them. There is nothing worse than trying to conduct a conversation or hold a meeting with the unspoken knowledge of differences which are accepted but kept covered. Get those differences out in the open and point out that not only are they there but that everyone knows they exist. They might be boss/employee differences or manager/client differences. Whatever the situation start from acknowledging the obvious. Then both sides can talk openly and more will be resolved.

4. Live up to people's expectations. If people expect someone in your position to walk through doors first then that is what you must do, even if it goes against your natural politeness. If you want to be respected in your position then you must behave as people expect someone in your position to do. If you don't, you will confuse people and they will be unsure about how to relate to you. A lot of your image is making sure that you live up people's expectations.

BOARD MEETINGS

When you arrive at a board meeting you must assess how your image fits in with the situation. If you arrive to find everyone in shirt sleeves or dresses then take off your jacket and become part of the group. This will make you acceptable to the group and your ideas will be better received. If you insist on remaining outside the situation by remaining completely formal in dress, then you will subconsciously be viewed as an outsider to the group and someone to be fought. In the same way you must tailor your method of working to each board meeting. If you find that it is very formally run with a strict form of address and code of working then you must accept it and adapt to it. If you find it is all first name terms and everyone chips in when they have something to say then you can be more relaxed. Again it is all about becoming acceptable. Because you are dealing not only with colleagues but your bosses you can take your cue from them.

DEPARTMENTAL MEETINGS

These are where you deal with your colleagues. Although the atmosphere may be more relaxed than board meetings you still need to persuade and get your ideas accepted. To do this you need to present an acceptable image to your colleagues – those whom you see every day and those you see less often in the course of your work.

You cannot go in and lay down the rules. But you can adapt your image to give yourself a better chance of persuading people that your ideas are the best. If you are too formal and stand-offish and want to try and lay down the law you will achieve nothing except antagonising the very people who may have to carry out whatever change of plan you may have in mind.

INTERVIEWING STAFF

This is a tricky situation. You may be interviewing with a team or on your own. However you do it you need to ensure that you do not confuse the interviewee. If you deviate too far from your usual work self then if and when the interviewees come to work for you they will arrive with completely the wrong impression of you. This will led to recriminations, uncertainty, fear and misery on their part, if not actual tears. You will not get the best work from someone who comes expecting, for example, a quiet, formal boss and who ends up with an outgoing informal one. People like to work with bosses with whom they think they have something in common. If you deceive them about your image then they will feel betrayed.

YOUR OWN INTERVIEW FOR PROMOTION

Now you are the one being interviewed. What should your image say about you? Again consistency is important. Your future boss wants to know what kind of person he or she is taking on. If you arrive at the interview in a wild red shirt and gold earrings and speak non-stop, and then turn up to work formally dressed and too shy to speak, then your boss will be disappointed and you will not make the progress you hope and expect.

Unless you are applying for an ultra creative position your should dress reasonably formally, if only to show that you are making an effort. Dress for the job above is sound advice but don't overdo it. If you dress exactly like the person you are taking over from, the interviewers may decide you have no personality of your own. The idea is to dress in the accepted style – a dress, not trousers, maybe, or a dark suit, not a light one. Try and have at least one more expensive accessory, perhaps a silk tie or a silver brooch to give your ensemble a lift.

Do not be afraid of voicing your ideas but don't adopt a matey attitude. Deference but confidence is the rule. Be prepared. Don't assume that because you are doing a job that you can be interviewed for the next rung up without doing your homework. There may have been changes since you last looked at it. If possible, talk to the person you are replacing or their colleagues and staff to find out what the up-to-date issues are.

If you are applying outside your present organisation then preparation is just as vital, if not more so. Again, be more formal than you might usually be. It is better to play safe rather than risk losing the job because you are determined to dress and behave *your* way, come what may.

TALKING TO YOUR TEAM

These are the people you have to motivate and lead to greater things. They will respect you for your knowledge of the job, your enthusiasm for the work, your ability to lead and support.

Dictatorial management styles are becoming things of the past. Encourage your staff to speak their minds about their work, your leadership, their colleagues. But make sure that the criticism is fair and not malicious. Inject a bit of humour into the situation. You need to listen to what your team has to say but at the same time it is your job to make the final decision about how and what work is done. You need to present an image to them that they will find acceptable and will encourage them to speak out and again to accept your decisions. Be encouraging, supportive and be prepared to delegate. Give your team members a chance to show what they can do. If you do the work 'because they're not ready' or 'I can do it quicker myself' then you are depriving them of a chance to learn and overburdening yourself. Your work will suffer and no-one will respect you. Let your staff do the work and a fair share of taking on new ideas. Support them and help them. They will pay you back tenfold. Discourage them and you will be seen as miserly and unresponsive – not a good image to send out to the world.

ADVISING SENIORS

You can take deference too far. If you are so scared of being disrespectful that you fail to put your ideas and opinions across, then you will be seen as a wimp and a coward and not somebody who is destined for the top. Don't be afraid of saying how you see it. But you can use more formal language than usual. 'That's rubbish!' may not go down well, whereas 'I don't actually agree that will work at this time because . . .' will get your point across firmly without becoming antagonistic or fresh.

Meeting the public

The occasions on which you need to meet the public are many and varied – meeting clients, fronting exhibitions, talking to local groups, dealing with complaints etc. How you deal with them will colour not only how the public perceives you but also your job and your company.

Do not be condescending or rude to members of the public. This may seem obvious but it is surprising how often this is done. The public are not fools and they do not take kindly to being treated as such. Rudeness does not only take the form of what is said but how it is said. It is perfectly possible to be scrupulously polite in your words but to convey a dislike of the person you are speaking to and also condescension. There is nothing in the words for the recipient to complain about but it can be devastatingly upsetting (you can tell I've had personal experience of this).

Don't ever do this. Not only is it unbelievably rude but it *will* get back to your firm, your boss and your colleagues. You cannot assume that a member of the public will be so cowed by you that they will not make sure it gets known by those who can deal with you. If the member of the public decides to complain by means of letters to the press or a radio phone-in, then your reputation is in ruins and your image at work will be zero.

However awkward, irritating, rude or unpleasant you find a member of the public *you* must behave impeccably. If you can help, do. If you can't, then find someone who can and make sure the name and message gets passed on. The public remembers the kind, polite person who tried to help, with gratitude.

WORD-OF-MOUTH MISCHIEF

Don't underestimate the power of word-of-mouth condemnation or praise. The chance remark in a greengrocer's, 'They're

65

useless at Z firm. Mrs Y was rude and unhelpful. Don't go there for your widgets' can ruin your firm and your own reputation, and may result in loss of business and take years to rectify. You may meet the public face to face in the course of your work in which case you must be as they expect you. You may be the world's best doctor but if you don't have a pleasant bedside manner and exude confidence in your diagnosis then people will not trust you to treat them.

Let's talk letters

Letters to colleagues take several forms: the formal letter outlining a policy decision or confirming the results of a meeting; an informal letter, perhaps inviting them to a work social event; a memo or a written note at the top of a document.

Courtesy in letter writing applies to colleagues as much as to anyone else. Spell words correctly. Use the greeting they find acceptable. Be clear about what you are saying. Even the informal note should be spelt correctly and be in legible handwriting.

Bad spelling is one of the most irritating things about receiving a letter from anyone. There is no excuse for it. Use a dictionary, even a 'bad speller's dictionary' if necessary. Or invest in a spelling machine (about the size of a small calculator). If you use a word processor beware of American usage. Many pieces of software come from the USA and you must make sure that any thesaurus or dictionary included is adapted for the UK English-speaking market. When your secretary types letters for you check the spelling. If it is incorrectly spelt it is your image, not hers, that will suffer. If she needs a dictionary or spelling software make sure she gets it.

Don't use slang or bad language in your letters. One day you will forget and send a memo to your boss couched in unsuitable terms!

When writing to the general public be courteous and helpful and again spell words correctly. People have great fun showing official letters to their friends and exclaiming 'No-one in XYZ firm can spell!' And your colleagues and boss will not think much of you if you spell incorrectly or write in an unintelligible scrawl. There are many books and classes for teaching handwriting so you have no excuse for writing illegibly.

When replying to complaints from the public do not immediately say 'It isn't our fault!'. Start by apologising for any mistake and then set out what can be done to rectify it. It is permissible to use humour where the situation warrants it and the problem is out of your control. For example, the Council officer's reply to worried mothers who had asked if swings, absent from the children's playground for three years, were ever going to be replaced: 'You may think the wheels of the Council grind exceedingly slow . . .' Too true, but it lightened the moment. The swings did get replaced in the end.

TELEPHONE MANNER

How you speak to people on the 'phone is a vital part of your image. The telephone is one of today's basic business tools and the ability to use it well will tell in your favour. At work you should answer the phone with:

- a greeting
- the name of your organisation
- your name
- your department if relevant

So it should be 'Good morning. Jane Blue of Zeddo company, Buying department speaking', not 'Hello'. The caller needs to know that they have reached the right organisation and department before continuing with the call. There are some professions such as social work, however, where there may be repercussions if the correct name is given. In that case using a pseudonym may be the answer.

Women professionals who work alone or apart from the main stream of the office can be vulnerable to obscene or terrifying phone calls. In this case the use of an answering machine may be sensible. This will allow callers to be screened. Otherwise a male assistant answering could help deter unpleasant callers. Obviously most women would prefer to answer their own calls, in which case make sure that you are aware how to contact BT quickly if the call becomes abusive. They can co-operate with the police to trace such calls and have methods of deterring future calls of a similar nature.

Keep calm if the caller is unhappy or angry. You can defuse the situation by:

- remaining polite
- apologising that the caller has had cause to complain at all
- listening carefully to find out the real problem and its extent
- offering your help where possible
- finding another source of help for the caller if you cannot help
- ensuring that a member of staff calls back at a later date to discover how far any problem has been rectified

Make sure that you speak clearly so that there is no possible way your words can be misinterpreted. Miss Jones of Sales can become Miss Bones of Wales if you are not careful.

How you answer the phone to your colleagues can make a difference to your image. Do you give your full name, your title and surname, just your first name? Give it some thought.

MAKE YOUR MACHINERY YOUR OWN

The mechanical aids of work life can be impersonal. For example, the fax machine will turn out the basic cover sheet provided by the company unless you take steps to change it. You can either take the company sheet and adapt it or create your own and instruct your secretary to use it on your behalf. Sometimes simply adding your name to the original version will suffice. Or you may want to make it more decorative and distinctive. Be careful, though. Your fax sheet should be distinctive, not overdone, and it should carry certain basic information besides the print information which the machine will automatically produce. The recipient will need to know:

- the number of sheets (including the cover sheet)
- the date (and possibly the time)

- the sender's name and address
- the sender's fax and 'phone number
- The organisation the sender belongs to
- who to reply to if different from the sender

Your company logo may suffice or you may want, say, the word FAX to be in a different type or to add a design. Be careful of funny pictures or copyright free pictures: they jar and are too common. Convey an image of efficiency and seriousness about work. Use a different size or weight of the same typeface (a fairly plain one will usually be sufficient). And you could head it with your own name prominently.

It is difficult to personalise a photocopied sheet. Coloured paper is not usually appropriate and photocopying is done on standard paper. You could, however, design a cover sheet to protect photocopies. A sheet with your name, company and telephone/fax number and the number of photocopies contained would suffice. If it had the company logo as well that would be better.

69

What the professionals say

Blackett Ditchburn. *Corporate Communications Manager for the Prudential Corporation plc*

The corporate communications department has a strong influence over every external communication that the company makes with the public at large. My responsibilities are for advertising, sponsorship, market research and community affairs, charity affairs, our library information service and government relations. We have a divisionalised structure in the UK and individual divisions may at times commission their own work. My job is to influence them in order to make sure that they do it within a reasonable corporate framework.

What image does the Prudential want to convey to the public? Absolute integrity and fair dealing, and that's pretty explicit. There is a reappraisal on at the moment and one of the things that we really want to keep is that idea of fair dealing and dealing with you, the individual, on a basis which with hindsight and knowledge, we think you would acknowledge as operating in your best interests. I think in comparison with our competitors we're winning that race.

The personal image of our people going out to the public is almost entirely how the public perceives Prudential. We're a service business. The opportunities the general public has to see and touch and experience Prudential are limited to advertising, brochures, and personal visits. Those visits and business conversations a lot of the time happen in the home, but to some extent may happen in offices of independent financial advisers. We don't have a shop you can go to and experience and put a finger on the quality. It's down to the individual face to face.

As far as my personal image is concerned, the first thing you get is an image of the advertising. The bulk of my association is with advertising, design, corporate identity, and they're supposed to be flash and a bit off the wall, anyway. So there's a background of prejudice before you even start. It's not necessarily destructive, it's just there.

The downsides of being in that particular category are usually accusations of being dilettante, of spending money rather than making pragmatic, sensible, meditated business decisions. One has to be aware that what will be in the forefront of people's minds is the accusation that you are being a bit thin and flaky. By and large it is a perfectly fair assumption. There are a lot of thin and flaky people in advertising and communications. If you're not happy with that then you have to try and become more thoughtful about it and try and present a much more reasoned case in all circumstances, appear to be more businesslike than people would have thought you were, and find opportunities to prove it to them.

I don't think I would alter my image in particular situations. I might stop swearing. But that's just being polite rather than changing my image. I feel quite strongly that one should not be untrue to oneself. I'm me and I should be natural in any environment. If you start doing that chameleon thing and saying 'oh, well, this is the certain kind of member of staff that one has to behave to like this', it would be a bit confusing because it's not going to be real and I think people can detect that.

The one thing that anybody who is going to regard you as the boss is scared about is a two-faced boss. You have to be absolutely straight down the line. If you try and behave one way to one person and one way to another you're going to split. They'll put two and two together. If you do it at interviews then it presumably means you're going to carry on doing it as and when they work for you. That would also erode trust.

I do think I behave in a slightly different way when I have to advise my superiors. Partly it's me personally. I don't trust bosses, but I've probably got it worse than most people and so I have a confidence problem to some extent with going upwards. I'm probably less ebullient with the boss. The further up the tree you go the bigger the egos get, the more particular become the terms, and they couldn't give a damn about 'what do you think?'. They are very confident and very consistent rather than chameleon. I suppose I am different but it takes a long time for me to get comfortable going upwards. In my particular circumstances, I'm asking them for decisions in a difficult area. It's only about eight years since the Pru took any of this communications 'nonsense' at all seriously. Therefore it's a difficult area for most senior managers who've been here for 20 years before that.

I don't put on a different suit or anything for my superiors. I think I alter the way I talk to them in the same way that I alter how I talk to people if I'm cross or praising. You don't get them in there with a big giggle on your face and say 'Hi, you're fired!' That just doesn't fit. I don't know if that's changing image. I will have much more serious conversations upwards. I'm unlikely to say to the chief executive, 'how was your beer at lunchtime?'. Maybe I should have done! I don't think people generally, people who work for me, or people who I've observed elsewhere, spend enough time thinking about the impact of their image. Their actions and their enthusiasm that they project up to me very much affects how much help and support they get from me. If someone starts playing the fool it's very hard to pull back and say 'look, you know they didn't mean it'.

You expose your ego more and more as you go up the tree and a lot of senior managers are extreme egoists as a defence mechanism. Again it's waves of suspicion or distrust coming up

71

because you have to be the author of tough decisions, to take people out, and however hard you try there's always going to be a legacy of doubt about your true motives. I don't think people realise that they get a bad boss as a consequence of projecting upwards a lot of bad vibes. It's a tough situation to be in but it's true. I think very few managers would admit it.

The Prudential does have courses on things called 'influencing skills' which I have to confess to being rather sceptical about. I think it's 99 per cent of the time a superficial waste of time. What they try to do is push you into a behaviour pattern that they tell you is good. I think it's much more important that you stay true to you. That comes from a caring boss actually coaching you over time saying 'look, you did this, now just back off a bit. What do you think of the consequence of that action?', rather than 'three days away and you'll come back reprogrammed with the perfect image'.

72

I think the important thing is that if somebody has a track record of doing things well, I couldn't care what they look like, how they behave or what they say to me. If they're doing things on my behalf and they try first time I would never want image to get in the way of that. You've got to have a track record of doing good work, and frankly if you're really good at doing what you're doing you can behave how you want, in my book.

When it comes to communications, I believe in our area people should express themselves, have a style. Answering the telephone should have standards attached to it. It should be done quickly and you should sound as if you're a person I want to talk to. One has a basic ethos of servicing people and trust. But as to a set form of words, you should do a bit better than 'hello', but then I'm the worst offender. As for writing, I would not do pro forma letters. I'd encourage people to be themselves, but I can understand where 'this is the way one does it' is a useful approach. Just writing a letter anyway you have a way of doing it, at least setting up the first paragraph if the letter is in response to something.

Do I personalise my fax sheets? I hadn't even thought about it. Maybe I should! There are managers who do that and they get their own notepaper printed. One has to be very cautious about it because it looks tinselly and pretentious. It's this double bind. As you get more senior as a manager your ego gets a thicker husk, you are making decisions within that, and you're less tuned into what people think as a consequence of that kind of gesture.

It's a language of gestures. Everything I say and do is a gesture to you, to anybody out there, or if this thing appears in print, it's a gesture to the reader about that 'pretentious git' who works at the Pru!

If you look at the really good managers they're often very good listeners, very low in the personality stakes. The high personality managers usually trip up. The good managers are sometimes very diffident, giving the impression they'd rather be reading a book than talking to people, but what they do is listen. The main thing is to keep rooting your image in reality. It's summed up in management by walkabout. Get behind the façade that's presented to you, figure out what people really think and then try and sort it out for them. An employee with a great track record of delivery I would let do anything, particularly in the creative area, and similarly I think a boss with a track record of doing things that seem to be in the majority interest can get people to do anything. But it works both ways. It's not really about image, though, it's more about how you operate.

I think one has to be aware that, particularly at times of stress, people will be suspicious of your own image. People who work for you have more time to talk about it and attribute motives to it. If you wear a new suit in a stressful moment it can lead to a rumour that you've been promoted. If you come in grumpy, because you've had a row with your wife, that won't be apparent to someone in the corridor. It would be 'God, he's in a bad mood. There must be some bad news coming'. You have to be real so that over time people begin to trust your actions. If your image is based on a track record of having delivered things right in the past they'll say 'well, he might be looking as if he's about to jump off the building this week, but maybe next week he'll give us the good news'.

My advice to aspiring managers would be to concentrate much more on doing a good job than worrying about your image. But recognise that it is at times more powerful than

73

doing a good job, though only just at times and in the long run it won't be. Concentrate conclusively on image and you may survive two or three projects and come out with shining colours, but sooner or later you'll be found out as being a bit shallow. So when at times it becomes more important than doing the job you've just got to be more sensitive as to when that is. I usually get it wrong!

LEARNING POINTS CHECKLIST

1 Adapt your image to different groups

2 Don't be offhand with people just because you are at work

3 Live up to people's expectations

4 Don't be a chameleon when interviewing staff or being interviewed

5 Remember that image is an important tool for persuasion

6 Don't be condescending or rude to members of the public

7 Check your spelling and make sure your handwriting is clear

8 Answer the phone with enough information to help the caller

9 Keep calm when talking to angry or upset callers

10 Personalise your fax or photocopies – but don't overdo it

74

DAY FOUR ACTION PLAN

Now that you know how important image is to your work you must set about changing it to make the best use of it. Take a look at your dress. Do you wear clothes acceptable to a large number of people? Are they adaptable? Do you wear or take a jacket to work that can be put on or set aside as the occasion demands? Go through your work wardrobe and put your clothes into adaptable working groups. Bear in mind that separates or suits in plain colours are more adaptable than lots of jazzy clothes. Plain clothes can be brightened up with accessories and can be made to look formal or informal, bright clothes nearly always look informal and are difficult to modify. Make a vital clothes list and decide to buy the ones you don't have:

1. Suit
2. Jacket
3. Several shirts
4. Alternative trousers or skirts
5. Two pairs of shoes
6. At least one classy accessory

Polish up your interviewing technique by interviewing your partner or a friend. Ask them to tell you if it is completely out of character.

Get a friend to interview you and ask the same questions. If you think that your skills need extra help decide to find a course in interviewing techniques. Write down what you usually say when you answer the phone. If it is uninformative write down what you should say and practise it. If necessary keep it on your desk at work as a reminder until it comes naturally.

If you come into contact with members of the public, make sure you are courteous and helpful. Do not give anyone cause to complain. Make sure you have a list of departmental 'phone numbers on your desk so that you can pass on callers to someone else if you cannot help them.

75

Look at a copy of a recent letter or memo you have sent at work. Is it presented nicely? Is it spelt properly? Is the recipient addressed correctly? If not, then correct it and double check your next letter.

Look at your fax header sheet and work out how to personalise it without going over the top. Can you add your name, change the type of your name or the word 'fax'? Does it contain all the necessary information? Design a better one and get your secretary to copy it neatly and use it. Do the same for your photocopy header sheet.

6

Impressing your customers

If you are in business the people you need to impress most are your customers or clients, both existing and potential. Without them there is no money, no business and no job for you.

You should now be aware how important your own image is, to how the outside world perceives both you and your job. If the customers like you, they will think better of your job; if they respect you, your profession will rise in their estimation.

This chapter tells you how to improve your image in the minds of your clients and customers. It discusses the situations in which you and your customers meet, and gives advice about what image you should be presenting and how.

Do the customers really care?

You may think that it doesn't matter what kind of image you are presenting to your customers. But then you cannot complain if you think that they undervalue your job and your own abilities. Why should they appreciate what you can do for them if you do not give the impression that you have confidence in it?

Customers want to think that they are valued and appreciated as individuals and that their needs merit your personal consideration. The person who may not necessarily have the most interesting job but whose manner to clients and customers suggests that he or she is concentrating solely on them and is interested in them will be more highly considered than the one who is offhand.

CARE ABOUT YOUR WORK

If you really care about your work then that enthusiasm will rub off and influence your client's view of you. If two people offer the same service at the same price the customer will go for the one who makes the customer feel that using that service will be pleasanter because the manager cares.

If you value your work but do not necessarily feel like clapping your hands for joy at the thought of it, then take a look at it. Ask yourself these questions:

- *Am I in the wrong job?* This is unlikely because otherwise you couldn't care about what your clients thought of you or the job. But if you really hate it then you should be looking for something else.

- *Is this just a dull patch?* It could be that your work is interesting most of the time and this particular project or job is necessary but dull. Keep up your enthusiasm by working on a more interesting future project in your spare time.

- *Are my colleagues or staff making work dull?* There is not much you can do about changing either of these groups of people for others. If one or two people are not pulling their weight and are dragging down the rest of the team then you may be able to transfer them elsewhere. Raise the enthusiasm of the group by brainstorming for new ideas and approaches to the work. Try to make people feel that their opinions and ideas are valued. By encouraging others your own enthusiasm will return.

- *Am I trying to do something I am not adequately trained to do?* If you have not adequately prepared for an aspect of your work or it is simply out of your area of expertise then, of course, the work will seem difficult and unenjoyable. Take time to discover courses or training which will fill in the gaps in your expertise. Not only will this be stimulating in itself but your approach to your work will be more informed and energetic as you feel able to cope with the work and new ways of tackling it occur to you.

- *You feel stressed about your work.* No job is enjoyable if you feel over-anxious, tired, panicky or even ill. Examine why

77

you feel this way. Is there simply too much work to do? Then you need to delegate more. Don't hog it. Give other people a chance to make a contribution. If you don't understand it then ask someone to help you. It is better to do that – there is no shame in it – rather than struggle on uncomprehendingly. If you actually feel ill then you must take time out to get better. It helps no one if you go in to work unable to concentrate and feeling wretched. Get better, then come in bouncing with health and enthusiasm. Is the deadline too close? Then ask for an extension or get more help. Don't suffer in silence.

By tackling the causes of your unenthusiastic response to work you can regain your enthusiasm and at the same time improve your way of working.

Which customers to impress

Some of your customers may be more important to you than others at the moment. The client with the major order every two months may be worth more financially to you than the small order every four months from a small company or individual. You may therefore think it sensible to concentrate on improving your image with the major customer.

This is a very short-sighted view. You can do this, of course, and no doubt your relationship with the major client will improve. But by ignoring your smaller customers you are laying yourself open to many dangers.

The first danger is that if you ignore the small fry the little orders will not be there to tide you over if the major customer goes under. The small ones could make the difference between saving yourself and disappearing with the big guys. Also, can you say with confidence that none of your smaller accounts will ever become major accounts? Won't you be sorry when that little company with the small order becomes much bigger and takes its custom elsewhere because you have undervalued them?

By taking time now to improve your image with *all* your

clients you are ensuring that you are laying down a customer loyalty which will stand you in good stead in the future. The minor customers will be there to support you during hard times and the major ones will boost your finances. And if that major company becomes a giant company, or that unassuming client becomes a key figure in a major concern, and they still use your services, then your efforts will have been well worthwhile.

The moral of this is that you cannot afford to let your image go in front of any customer because your reputation and the view they will have of your work could affect how they treat you in years to come.

Related customers and companies talk to each other as well. Their managers get together at conferences, their staff meet in the street, bosses in a similar line of business get on the 'phone to each other. If your image is tarnished for one company you could be tarnishing it with all related companies for a long time to come. The same is true of people. If your customers are individuals, not companies, then if they are in related areas of work they will talk to each other or read comments in their trade or professional journals and they will soon get to know if you have treated one person less thoughtfully than another. So you cannot take the risk. You must build your reputation and that of your job on all-round quality at all times to all people.

79

WHO ARE YOUR IMPORTANT CUSTOMERS?

It should be clear from what I have just said that all your customers are important. But there may be a few occasions, and only a few, when you do need to project your image in a different way to certain customers. These are:

1. A customer is planning to take his or her business elsewhere.
2. You have been promised work if you change certain aspects of your image.
3. You think that the image you are portraying to your customers is out of date.

Much will depend on how important you think the customer is. If they are long-standing and prompt payers and you think that their loss would be very detrimental then you should consider altering your image to keep them.

On the other hand, if they have been more trouble than they are worth (and even major clients can be this) then let them go and keep your present image intact. Sometimes a customer's demands are so time-consuming and demanding that you are expending far more time and energy on their needs than their custom warrants. A loss in income might occur if they left you but you may gain more by having extra time for other customers and time to concentrate on attracting new business. And don't underestimate the value of your peace of mind and health. If you do decide that they need to be persuaded to stay find out what it is about your image that they don't like. If the quality of your service is fine but they don't want to be associated with you because your image is outdated then you should seriously consider means of bringing it up to date. This is something you should consider at regular intervals anyway. Even firms and individuals who deliberately project a 'traditional' image need to add those extra touches keep them up to date.

In the same way that a firm can subtly alter its logo, bring in discreet but essential technology or tailor its uniforms slightly differently, so you as an individual can make those updating touches which will bring the recognition factor into play. You want your clients to recognise you as providing a good service and reliable but also up to date. Look at what you can do:

- alter your own dress with an up to date collar line, different shoulder width, modern colours, modern hemline, modern haircut.
- invest in technology such as a fax, photocopier and answering machine (how did you survive without them?)
- alter office stationery
- bring telephone training for all staff up to date so that the customer gets a bright helpful response
- improve response time to letters, faxes and phone calls
- send more individuals out to meet clients
- meet more of the customers yourself

- respond more to your customers' needs

All these things may seem obvious but it is surprising even now how many companies and the people within them take customers for granted and are happy to continue in the same old way. Yet it may only take a few simple alterations to bring the customers back and happier than before.

Have you been letting your service slide? Whether you are a professional working on your own or part of a large company the service you offer should be the best you can provide all the time. And the service you give one customer should be the service you give another.

If customers say to you for example, 'I'm going elsewhere with my custom unless you make your image more acceptable to young mothers', then you should seriously consider why they are saying this. Is it because you do not try to attract young mothers to use your business at all? Is it because young mothers do use your services but you do not make an effort to entice them? Do any young mothers who use your services find it unsatisfactory?

If you have a client who wants to make sure that using your services will associate his or her business with one which young mothers find attractive, then if you want to keep that customer you are going to have to accommodate him or her. Are your staff sympathetic to young mothers? Does your advertising attract them? Are there ample facilities in your premises for them? Do you go out and talk to young mothers to find out what they want? Are you dressed and do you behave in a way which young mothers would find reassuring and helpful?

Making slight but necessary alterations in these areas could mean that you keep your customer and at the same time attract new custom.

How to make your clients love you

Your clients and customers are going to love you for certain things:

- excellent service or products

- reliability
- reasonable cost
- speed of service
- individual attention
- pleasant approach by individuals in the firm
- a modern image
- an excellent aftercare service
- that indefinable something that makes you different

You may say that you and your company provide this anyway and that your customers seem quite happy, thank you. But take a closer look. Aren't there a few things you are missing? Take a look at each of the points in turn in relation to your own image. Are there ways in which you can improve them in any ways, however small?

If you are perfect you are lucky, but I suspect that there is room for improvement on all counts. And it may be only slight differences that will change your image and that of your work completely in the eyes of your customers.

An individual who after years of sending out letters suddenly sends out a classy fax within the hour certainly improves his or her image of speed and efficiency and the image of work goes up in customers' perceptions.

The manager who takes time out to meet some of his customers personally is improving his or her own image and that of his firm.

The professionals who take time to make that phone call to find out whether their clients are satisfied with their services are improving their image and that of their profession.

The organisation which provides facilities for the elderly while they are waiting is improving its image.

Out and about

Your potential customers and your existing ones are out there together. If you don't meet them how can you impress them with your image and instil in them an impression of a good image of your work? This is where you have to become your own salesperson to the public.

What opportunities do you have or can you make for meeting the public? These can be directly related to your work such as business lunches or conferences or they can be more informal such as talks to groups or showing visitors around. Let's look at some of these in more detail.

TALKS

Local or national groups often ask people with particular expertise to come and talk to them. This can be as basic as police constables, ambulance drivers or fire-fighters going into a local school to tell the children what they do or as formal as addressing a large national organisation on the specifics of your work.

Take the opportunity to give such talks when they are offered. It is an ideal opportunity to go out and meet the public and your customers and to impress your image upon them. If you have not been invited to give such talks you can offer your services. Many organisations are delighted to have speakers and some even offer expenses! Try local political groups or sections of them, such as the women's or black sections, traditional venues such as the Women's Institute or Townswomen's Guilds, Rotary Clubs, schools, clubs. If you have enough expertise and time you could give adult education classes or Workers' Educational Association (WEA) classes in your job.

Do not overlook talking to children. Not only are they your future customers (or staff!) but they exert a powerful influence over their parents and guardians. If they want to go to Mr Green the dentist because he was so nice when he talked to them at school, Mr Green may well end up with more clients. Conversely, if they refuse to go near Dr Clark because he was brusque with them you may have trouble getting any of the family through the surgery door again. Don't talk down to children but make sure that you explain everything in a way they can understand. Talk clearly and wear clothes which, although in keeping with your work, mean that you can get down to the same level as little ones or join in activities with older pupils without fearing for your dignity or your clothes.

If you or your firm can arrange for children to visit your workplace, this is much enjoyed by the pupils and staff and impresses the parents no end. As a parent myself I have never sat in a fire engine, visited police stables or seen a newspaper put to bed. But I am most impressed with the organisations that arranged for my children and their fellow pupils to do so.

Adults and children alike need humour injected into any talk. Not only does it keep them awake but it makes you seem more approachable and sympathetic. Beware, though, of pitching jokes for the adults in a group of children and adults. That is patronising and will not endear you to the younger members of the audience. When talking to adults do not be afraid of mentioning the less glamorous parts of your work or times when you made a mistake. Everyone loves to know that other people aren't perfect and respects people who can admit to that and yet seem successful. It gives us all hope.

84

CONFERENCES

There are many kinds of conferences. They can be for colleagues in the business, suppliers, customers or the general public. When they are for clients or the general public, then this is your big chance to make an impression. Typically conferences will consist of talks during all or part of the day with dinner and/or social activities in the evening.

You, I hope, will be giving a talk. If you haven't been asked to do so, you can volunteer. Particularly if you have some important aspect of your work which will otherwise not be covered at the conference.

How should you dress for talking at a conference? Dress smartly but comfortably. Look as if you know what you are doing. But adapt to the audience. If the audience is a very formal group of Japanese businessmen or conservatively-dressed accountants then dress accordingly. If however, it is filled with, for example, advertising copywriters, in more casual and exotic clothes, take off your jacket and tie or literally roll up your sleeves and gain more empathy with the audience. Talking to an audience is more than just standing there with your hands at your sides. What you have to convey is an enthusiasm for your subject, so convey it in a way that your audience understands and appreciates. There are some key points to remember:

1. *Know your subject.* If you don't know enough about it you will founder and the audience will sense your unease. Prepare well beforehand.
2. *Adapt to your audience.* Don't talk in technicalities to the general public or in general terms to a group of industry expects.
3. *Speak clearly.* 'Speak to the clock at the back of the room'. Check the microphone beforehand if one is used.
4. *Make some jokes.* They don't have to be complicated and they can gently mock yourself. They must not be offensive. People like humour from their speakers.
5. *Use illustrations – slides, projections, film – where possible.* This makes it easier for you to remember and interests the audience. Prepare by speaking at home in time to the slides and make sure you can master the technicalities.
6. *Do not have too much to drink beforehand.* One glass of alcohol may relax you. Two or more may make you at best slightly off-key and at worse too inebriated to give the talk properly. Think what *that* will do to your image!
7. *If the audience wants to ask questions take them at the end.* Make your answers honest – if you don't know, say so.

I go into more detail about presentations and talks in the next chapter.

You may be going to a conference, not as a speaker but as a listener in order to further your own or your company's image. Your role then will be to participate as a member of the audience.

You may think that it is difficult to do much about projecting your image from a seat in the hall. But it is not only the people on the stage who can command attention. If you can, position yourself near the front, but not in the front row. Listen carefully to what the speakers say and when they ask for questions have one ready. Do not try to be too clever but ask one that sounds intelligent. 'I was interested in your theory about . . .

Could you explain how that relates to . . .?' Try to ask the first question if possible. Companies like their representatives to show their faces and many encourage them to use such tactics because it gets the company's image in front of a large audience, especially if you say 'I'm Bob Brown from XYZ company' and then ask your question.

Occasionally, if the conference is an important one it will jog a reporter into making note of you and your question or a television camera may home in on you, especially if it looks as if the answer will be interesting. If you are working for yourself you can use the same tactics. This time, however, you would announce yourself, for example, as 'Mary Smith, consultant psychiatrist'.

Make the most of the opportunity to introduce yourself to as many people as possible after the lectures, either in the bar, over a meal or at any social and cultural events. Networking should take place as much as possible and is one of the main points of conferences.

Although most people will be wearing name badges at any properly-run conference you may find it difficult to remember names. And it does not seem polite to keep leaning forward and peering closely at someone's name badge. To help you remember names remember these rules:

1. When told someone's name always repeat it immediately as in 'Pleased to meet you, John'
2. Use the name again as soon as possible in the conversation for example ' That's interesting, Mary, do you often find . . . ?
3. Associate the person with some memorable characteristic in your mind so that 'John Black is the man from marketing with the red spectacles and 'Mary Green is the woman from XZY Company with silver hair'
4. Immediately you return to your room write down a list of the people you met and wish to recall together with the characteristic you associated with them
5. Do not lose any business cards: annotate them with useful details as soon as you can

YOU *ARE* THE FIRM AT FUNCTIONS

You may well attend many functions such as sports events, social events, inter-company events as a representative of your firm or your profession. How well you do so will dictate how well your own image is perceived as well as that of your firm.

Do not turn down too many opportunities to represent your firm. It is a good chance to keep in the public's eye and to enhance yourself in the eyes of your bosses. After all you wouldn't have been chosen if they had not thought you were suitable and would be a credit to them.

Do your preparation. Nobody's image is enhanced by arriving at any function unsure of what it is for and why they are there. You need to know:

1. Exactly what the function is. For example, if it is a social event, what kind of social event
2. Who will be there
3. When it will be held and more importantly perhaps, what time it finishes, so that you do not overstay your welcome
4. What dress is expected. Will it be dinner jacket and evening dress or white tie or less formal?
5. How does your firm expect you to dress?
6. What arrangements have been made? Is there more than one venue? How do you get there? Have seating, badges, folders been arranged?
7. Who do you reply to?
8. Who is in charge?
9. If there is a talk prepared what questions would your company like answered?
10. Who are the most important people to meet?

Make sure that you have accepted in good time and know what the arrangements are and are dressed appropriately. If that means getting your dinner jacket or evening dress cleaned do so well beforehand. Read about the subject of any talk if there is one and make sure that you are aware of who will be attending and what they do and their importance or relevance to the firm. If you are representing yourself or a profession the same rules apply but you must find out who is useful for you to know in an individual capacity.

87

Even if you are naturally shy this is not the time to stand in a corner. Your image depends on being open and friendly at functions and being willing to listen to other people. You may find many people there boring or irritating but they may be of importance to you or your company. Do not show your dislike.

BUSINESS LUNCHES

Business lunches can be anything from a snack with a colleague at the local pub to a grand meal for a dozen people in the boardroom. Your image on these occasions must match the occasion. With a colleague or friendly opposite number from the company you can be relaxed and more casual. With a more formal group you must be friendly but not take over the conversation. Whatever the size of the lunch you must remember that a business lunch is just that, to further business. You can indulge in social chit-chat to some extent (and you will have a dour image if you can't) but you must be prepared to discuss the business in hand and come to some agreement. The days of the heavy business lunch seem to be rapidly disappearing. In today's fast-moving world we cannot afford to eat and drink a great deal at lunchtime and sink down unable to do much for the rest of the afternoon. Nor can we afford to take three hours over our lunch – you can be sure your competitors won't. So if you indulge in heavy meals and lots of drink your image will suffer. You will be marked down as someone who is not going to move in the fast lane and is not worth talking to. Other less indulgent people will be eating lightly and leaving early and stealing a march on you.

Over-indulgence in drink at a business lunch is probably one of the worst sins. If you drink too much you will not be able to concentrate well, may be indiscreet and may indulge in unacceptable behaviour. If in doubt stick to one glass of alcohol and mineral water. Nobody will think anything about you drinking water because most people do nowadays. It will show that you want to stay alert and pay attention to what people have to say.

VISITORS

You may be asked to show visitors around your company or decide to show people round your work place. Here again your image comes into direct contact with the public. If you are only taking a brief time out from your job to do this then you can be in your working clothes but they must be clean and tidy. If you are spending all day showing people around then you will be expect to dress more formally. Make sure that all safety regulations are complied with and that you do not patronise your visitors. People take a genuine interest in how other people do their jobs. They may not understand them but that does not mean that you can treat them as fools.

Show enthusiasm for your workplace and a pride in it. It is you who will be remembered, not that brief glimpse of the Chief Executive in the distance. Your friendly manner, pleasant way of answering questions, enthusiasm and energy is what will remain in the visitors' minds. If you can impress this on them then they will think of your job in the same light and the firm will benefit. But it is your name they will carry away with them. 'We were shown round by Mrs Robinson. She was ever so friendly.'

89

DINNERS

Dinners are more formal than business lunches and you should dress accordingly. Again beware of heavy drinking and arrange for a taxi or a lift home if necessary. Listen carefully about how to address people. If you are already on first-name terms with the other diners then you have no problem. But if in doubt, especially to more senior people and people from other companies, then use their titles until you are aware that first-name terms are acceptable. Usually you will get 'Betty, please', after the first formal mode of address but many senior people will prefer to be called by their title and preserve a slight formality. Your image will not be enhanced if you bounce into the room and call everyone by their first name whoever they are. You will merely be thought bumptious and juvenile and not worth bothering with. That does not mean you have to be serious the whole time but keep your levity under control. No jokes about a rival company if their representative is standing just behind you!

MEETING VIPs

Don't assume you will never meet a VIP. This could be someone in your company, for example, the Chairman who has just been knighted or the lady from catering who is an Olympic Gold medallist in swimming. You may meet pop stars on a publicity stunt, TV stars using your company grounds for a film, royalty on a visit or the local mayor presenting merit awards. You may not approve of all or any of the many versions of VIPs whom you may meet in the course of your work but do not let that show. The mere fact that they have visited will do wonders for publicity for your firm and if you get to meet them can do wonders for your own image.

Dress respectably, be respectful, laugh at their jokes and explain your job or the company pleasantly. If there is a photographer or a reporter or TV cameras around standing near to the VIP, this will not harm you! You may meet VIPs as you go out from your job either in social situations, in your private life or when out and about for your firm. Again, do not be rude to them whatever you think of them. That would do your image no good at all.

What the professionals say

Joy King. Head of Public Relations, Manweb plc

Manweb's image is about how the public views us. We've done some in depth research recently. We were under the impression that most people felt they knew us quite well and that they were quite favourably inclined towards us. But what transpires is that there's a latent hostility towards Manweb that people don't realise they have. It's there because Manweb is one of the organisations that provide what the customer sees are essential, life-giving services that the customer has no control over.

What we're trying to do is to change everything that we're doing in terms of how we communicate with customers and the public, to ensure that customers feel that we are talking to them in a tone which is not patronising, but which is friendly, more advisory, which is trying to give them advice that will help them make the right decision and put them in control so they can make the decisions themselves. It's all about how we speak to them, the way that we speak to them and increasing the choice that they have.

We want to be seen as a professional organisation that gives customers choice, and everything that we do will be of the highest quality so that customers can trust us. But it has also to be the most cost-effective service. So that is how we're trying to position ourselves, as a high quality, low cost utility provider.

One of the most important things in my view is the consistency of message right across the company. You don't change the message, you tailor it for different audiences. So the message is tailored, but it's tailored in how you communicate, not what you communicate.

I want to be seen as a professional doing the very best job that anybody can do so they can say 'She is one of the best PR people in the industry in the country'. That's how I want to be seen because that reflects on the company and that's how I want the company to be seen – as one of the best companies in the country. Because you're in such a high profile role, it is important that you convey that impression to people but you can't do it on a glossy surface point of view. You have to mean it, and it also has to be backed up with real solid facts and other things that you can use to present yourself professionally.

I set about presenting a professional image by being well prepared. When I have meetings with people I know the messages that I need to get across, what I'm hoping to achieve with that meeting. A lot of what I do is really building relationships and keeping the relationships in place so that when we need them we have a trusted relationship with an individual. You're building an existing relationship, so you're not needing to build on that when you've got a crisis.

We have a corporate identity manual which says you should use the corporate logo and the company name. We don't have a set of rules. We do psychometric testing of new people when we bring them in and there is a company culture that we're trying to get across to people in a lot of training at the moment. But it's not written down as such and I don't think it ever will be because the company is evolving so fast I can't imagine setting down a set of rules that are going to be right because they'll change straight away. Anyway I suspect that the chief executive wouldn't like it because it's not our style. We're not a bureaucratic organisation and rules and rule books are somewhat frowned upon. The initiative of the individual is definitely to be encouraged.

I don't think I tailor my own image to different groups of people. Even on those occasions when I go into schools it's still basically me. So I don't consciously change myself. I don't think I change myself unconsciously, either. The messages that I'll be giving out, the way I'll be saying things will be different but I don't think that will change the professional approach.

I think my personal image does cause people to form an opinion of the company and that is the professional quality without a shadow of a doubt. So does the image of the chief executive and the senior directors of the company, which is one of the reasons why I get the job of telling people to have their hair cut. I'm very unpopular and if they're not dressing correctly it's terribly important. It's all about people's perceptions and you're not dealing with reality, reason or logic, you're dealing with how people think about other people.

Everybody compartmentalises people. The way I run my business life is because of the expectations of other people. The City is one of the most old-fashioned institutions in the whole country, as is the House of Commons, and I have to deal with both. I look after Parliamentary affairs and investor relations, so you have to fulfil their expectations. If the chief executive went down to London in a brown suit, or had a pony-tail, it would be disastrous for this company. He would not be taken seriously. It wouldn't matter what he said. It indicates the shallowness of some aspects of human life which I find absolutely appalling, but nevertheless you have to recognise it's there. It's no good fighting it. You can't change that, it's only going to harm the company and all the time we've got to think what is the best for the company, even if it goes against the grain.

You have to have a solid base because that's underneath the gloss. If people get conflicting messages between what you're doing and what you're saying then the image just breaks down. If I was going around reacting in a way which wasn't me somebody would see through it.

I came in at this level in the company and I'm still in this role but I have progressed in the company. Partially it's about presentation but it's also about execution. A lot of what I achieve is not seen because if you're really good at PR you achieve things in subtle ways so that people don't always realise it's something that you've instigated. There's a lot of subterfuge, subtlety, and lateral thinking about how you achieve something.

It ultimately boils down to how reliable you are, how much of what you've advised, what you've said, or what you've done in the past, has been right. I don't go in to the chief executive and say, 'you've got to do this because it's absolutely wonderful!'. He's going to have his back up straightaway and the first thing he's going to say is, 'why on earth should I do that?' I'm talking about a much greater level of preparedness in how you achieve things. The obvious thing is how you put forward a suggestion.

Have I consciously changed my image? Four years ago I decided I wasn't going to wear any more dark suits. I suppose there really only were dark suits available at that time. But brighter suits, more feminine clothes and colours, had started coming in and I thought, 'why should I dress in black all the time. Just because men wear black suits and pinstripe suits, why should I?' So I don't. It was just something I felt like doing at the time. It was a statement and I was keen to encourage other women. But I can't imagine myself changing radically. I've got to live with myself, that's the important thing to me. I'm not going to change the way I do something. I might bite my tongue a bit more when I might have had a good old go at somebody. It's more in my nature to have a really good old go. I don't suffer fools gladly so I'm afraid I sometimes find that I have to bite my tongue because I know it's going to harm the company if I say something. So, yes, you do find yourself

93

wishing you could do something and knowing that you can't because it would harm the company. We've definitely changed our image in response to the customer. The way we present ourselves, the tone and the things that we're saying, we've consciously changed that. It's a direct result of their innermost feelings towards the company.

Personal image is important in relation to company image. If I was doing everything wrong or I wasn't thought of very highly, that would affect the company. But it wouldn't be the be-all and end-all. If everybody in the company was doing everything wrong then that would seriously affect the company. You've only got to look at some of the companies in this sector who are doing damaging things to their image. If you take that to its ultimate conclusion, the company isn't valued correctly and somebody will come in and make a bid for it, so the company will no longer exist. That is all down to perception in the City. The City has got nothing to differentiate electricity companies by at the moment. It's still a new area. So what they do is they look at the strategy that's being communicated, they look at the people in the company and they take a view on the management strength.

Management strength is the key thing and then their strategies and their communicating. What are the things that link those two things? It's all about the consistent messages and its all about how they are communicating. It's all about the perception of the image of the company and that's what makes the difference between the top one and the bottom one. My advice is don't ever lose your sense of humour. It helps enormously. Humour is very important because people don't like companies or people who take themselves too seriously.

I think an area we've not discussed yet is why image is important. In the region, it's all about new business opportunities coming and it's about survival. If the general public like people who work for Manweb, they like the way you treat them, with professionalism, then they are going to view Manweb as a whole as a company they want to deal with. That's the main objective.

One of the things we're focusing very hard on is that we want our customers to think favourably of us because we're going to be introducing new services. We want them to think of Manweb first. So the way we're seen in the region is vitally important to us. We spent a lot of time making sure that we're involved in the region, that we put money into new enterprise agencies to get businesses to come into the region, to get the community working, and we do that deliberately, again to make sure that the region feels that Manweb is an integral part of it, and it's doing a lot of good for the company and us. That's what we want the region to be saying about Manweb. There's going to be a situation where things will change. We want that loyalty.

You cannot build an image overnight. It takes a lot of effort, over a long time, and you've got to be consistent. It's all about consistency. That's another thing about people who do things in an area and then they pretend it's all for altruistic reasons and don't want their name to be mentioned. I can't understand that at all. That's not professionally correct, it's a nonsense because there are good sound commercial business reasons why you should want to project your image into the region. People aren't fools. They're happier if you say, 'well, we'd like to have some recognition'. We want return for that investment and I just don't believe these people who say it's all altruistic.

You've got to get on with people you don't like. You shouldn't be in PR unless you can. Anyone who can will do well. You want people to say, 'I like you, I like the management, I like the company.' That's what you want everyone to say. If you can do that you've probably achieved a good part of PR.

95

LEARNING POINTS CHECKLIST

1 Remember *all* your customers are important

2 Never patronise your customers

3 Show enthusiasm for your job

4 Give the customers what they want

5 Deliver the best service or product possible

6 Take the opportunity to meet the public when you can

7 Preparation is the key to giving successful talks

8 Network as much as possible

9 Don't drink or eat too much at business lunches or dinners

10 Don't be rude to VIPs

DAY FIVE ACTION PLAN

Day five is the day you should use for preparing to meet the general public including your clients. Write down a list of your clients and star those you consider most important with the reasons. List as many ways as possible that you could improve your image and the image of your job and company. Include:

- standard of product or service
- reliability
- speed of service
- pleasantness of service
- telephone response
- modern equipment
- things customers themselves have asked for

Are there any particular *groups* of customers that you are not fully catering for? List the ways you could change to help them.

Star three ways to change your image and your job's image tomorrow, e.g. discuss improved telephone response with switchboard and secretary, send for catalogues of fax and photocopying equipment, alter delivery timetables. Check your diary for dates when you will be meeting the public. If there are none discuss the opportunity to do so with your boss.

Write down a list of things you need to know for each occasion and where you can get the information from. Obtain the information either today or tomorrow and prepare carefully. Arrange to give a talk to a local group about your work. Write down what you usually drink and eat at business lunches and dinners. Work out how you can change your meals without seeming rude, e.g. substitute mineral water for some of your drink, have a salad instead of vegetables for some meals, have fruit instead of dessert, use a sweetener for your coffee.

7

Presentations

It is possible to create an image for yourself without ever meeting people – Howard Hughes did so – but the result could be more negative than positive and you would find it difficult to correct any misconceptions.

Ideally you need to meet people face-to-face and impress them with the charm of your personality and your enthusiasm and ability. By meeting you they will be able to form their own impression about your suitability for a job, your reliability as a supplier or trustworthiness as a colleague. One of the most powerful ways of making face-to-face contact with people is by making presentations.

Presentations are occasions when you stand up in front of an audience and give a talk about your work, your product or your company. It could be a presentation to a few of your colleagues about the progress of your work so far or about new proposals; to the entire directorial team about the progress your section is making; to an audience of hundreds of your opposite numbers in the industry about what your company is doing, or any number of in-between occasions.

What these occasions all have in common is that you have to stand up in front of an audience and explain something in a way which the audience will understand and which will interest and inspire them. As you will be the centre of attention your image is a vital part of the presentation process. It is also an excellent opportunity to enhance your image in the eyes of key people in your area of work. Even if the content is good, they will not be impressed if it is poorly presented by somebody who has not taken image into account. Conversely, if the content is poor but it is well presented by someone who strikes a chord with a sympathetic image, then you will be remembered but as that exciting person who wasn't quite up to the job. 'Wonderful personality, shame about the talk'.

This chapter will guide you through the hazards of making presentations and will show you how proper preparation and consideration of audience attitudes will help you give a presentation in the best possible way so that your image will be enhanced.

Talking is image

Don't believe anyone who tells you that what you say and how you say it doesn't matter as long as you do the work. We are sociable animals who use words as the most important means of our communication. We judge people on how they speak, what they say and how they say it. It may be a subconscious reaction and barely noticeable in most people but it is still there.

We may say that we are not prejudiced by the way people speak but if pressed we will say that we like people who speak clearly and are reasonably polite in their language, that we approve of people who can explain things well without being patronising and enjoy a bit of humour. We like accents but want to understand what is being said. All this boils down to the concept of clarity of communication. No one nowadays is going to worry if you have a strong accent or don't speak BBC or 'the Queen's' English. But both those concepts had a basis in good manners. That is, what was said had to be immediately understandable to anybody who used English as their language of communication. (The same principle of course applies to other languages used in other countries.)

This meant that there had to be common ground. Words in common currency only in one part of the country could not be used because they would not be understood in another part. Accents were discouraged because they were considered a hindrance to people's understanding, however slight the accent. The result was that there was a common standard of language which enabled communication to take place in any part of the English-speaking world, with the result that the listener and the speaker both understood the same thing.

Nowadays we are more relaxed. Accents are permitted, even encouraged, as long as they are not so strong that people have difficulty in understanding what is said. In fact, we now welcome the cultural diversity of sound without which our language would be a dull monotone. We do not demand a rigid use of grammar because some changes have become acceptable over time even to the pundits, for example 'There's lots of ducks' instead of 'There are lots of ducks'. But we expect a reasonable standard of grammar to aid comprehension.

We allow the use of unusual regional words as long as they are immediately understandable or have become part of the mainstream of language. We encourage humour and welcome enthusiasm in speech as long as the speaker does not babble, but the basics of good communication remain the same and your image depends on your ability to incorporate these aspects into your everyday speech and presentation language. They are:

99

- clarity
- good grammar
- honesty
- acceptable language
- sincerity
- enthusiasm
- humour

If you lack all or some of these attributes in your speech then you are allowing your image to be tarnished. You can only present an acceptable image and impress other people if they are fully aware of what you are trying to communicate and are persuaded to agree with it. This depends on language.

How you speak also plays a part. If you are dishonest in what you say nobody will trust you. Don't think you won't get found out – you always will. If you are unpleasant or rude then you will be disliked and mistrusted. 'If she says that about her, what does she say about me when I'm out of earshot?' If you are unenthusiastic, why should anyone give you the extra work? If you gabble, nobody will bother to listen after the first few minutes, nor will they if you speak in a slow monotone. A combination of how you speak and what you say is the most powerful image tool. When you meet the press, as I discuss in the next chapter, your words may no longer be ephemeral but recorded for all to ponder over. If you say it in the wrong way it is there for all to see or hear.

Don't be two-faced

It is no good having ability to use language well if you are dishonest in your use of it. That does not mean necessarily lying, but being unable to match what you are saying to what you actually do.

When you first speak to people they are going to take a lot about you at face value. If your outward image is acceptable and you sound sincere they will trust you, at least to begin with, to do what you say you will. Be sure that you match what you say to what you do. If you say that your company is reliable and always delivers the goods on time and yet again and again the orders arrive late or not at all your credibility rating will plummet. If you say that you will do something for someone and then fail to do it you will not be believed the next time. If you expound the quality of your service or product and it then fails to live up to your fine words you will not be trusted again.

You must be prepared to do what you say you will do and to be honest about what you can and can't deliver in the way of work, services or products. It is far better to be honest to start with than to backtrack later. People will respect you more and feel able to make a more sensible appraisal of what you have to offer.

SINCERE SPEECH

When you give presentations you must be equally clear in what you say. You must be straightforward and honest. Forget about trying to fool your audience. When they find out, and they always will, they will not think you clever. They will instead think you devious, tricksy and untrustworthy.

100

Be equally honest when you answer questions. It is far better to admit that you don't know and that you will find out something than make something up or give a half-truth. Being 'economical with the truth' has now passed into folklore as the most laughable of language tricks. Admit your mistakes, your ignorance and fallibility and you can come back later with improvement. If you start by being devious, you will not be allowed to come back.

That does not mean that you should not present yourself in the best light possible. But you can do that without lying. Present the positive side of your life but be honest when you should be.

Talented talking

When you are asked, or decide, to give a presentation on any scale you must first find out who you are to give it to and decide what you want to say. Both these things are vital. It is no good preparing a detailed technical analysis of your latest project only to discover that you are speaking to a group of salespeople who only want you to tell them the broad sales points. Nor would it be helpful to produce a short, lightweight talk about 'funny things that happen in the office' for a meeting of scientific advisors. So first find out:

1. Who is your audience to be?
2. What are they expecting to hear about?
3. Where will the presentation take place?
4. When will it take place?

Once you have sorted out the basic details you can then start to plan your presentation.

First be honest with yourself. Are you the best person to give the talk? If you do not know enough about the subject nor can find out, if you will not be able to get to the venue on time, if you actually feel ill if you have to make presentations, then you are not the best person to do so. Hand it over to a colleague, a member of your staff or decline. Don't try to do what you can't.

Most people can give talks if they prepare properly. There are a number of important things you must do:

1. Know your subject
2. Prepare thoroughly
3. Check any illustrations
4. Visit the venue if possible
5. Check any equipment
6. Practise using any equipment
7. Practise your speech
8. Dress appropriately

If you do all this then your presentation will go well.

KNOW YOUR SUBJECT

The worst thing you can do with any presentation is to stand up without having properly researched what you are going to say. You may think that you do not need to prepare because you are involved in the work every day. But when you stand up and talk to an audience you must know, if not everything, at least everything that your audience might want to know. Remember that most presentations end with the opportunity for the audience to ask questions and so you must know enough not only to give your talk, but answer any enquiries afterwards.

First find out what the audience *expects* to hear. This may have been decided for you. If the organisers of the event have slotted you into a programme then they may well have asked you to 'talk about the technical aspects of your job'. If you are not sure what is wanted then ask the organiser. Find out, too, how long you will be expected to speak for. That will help you decide how much detail you can fit into your talk.

If the organiser or you are unsure of what should be in the talk then find out who your audience will be. This will give you some idea of what is wanted and what level to pitch your talk at. It will also give you an idea of how formal the occasion is likely to be. If you are giving a presentation to your colleagues you may be able to provide coffee and sandwiches and roll your sleeves up and allow interruptions. If you are to speak to a group of senior executives then you may be more formal.

PREPARE THOROUGHLY

Now that you know roughly what your talk should be about you must start your preparation. Give yourself as long as possible to do so. The better prepared you are, the less nervous you will be and the more the audience will appreciate your talk. Start by writing notes about the subject – everything you know from your own experience. Then get as many up-to-date books, articles and papers on the subject as possible. You may have been happily continuing your work in your own way but other people may have other opinions and ideas. Even if you don't agree with them you should be able to refer to later thoughts on the subject and dismiss them if necessary. In any case, someone from the audience is bound to ask you about the latest opinion on your subject.

When you have gathered all the information start to write your speech. Use lots of headings and subheadings as guides to your talk. Unless you are experienced in public speaking take the time to write the whole talk out to begin with. Then read it out in front of a mirror to gauge the amount of time it will take. This may seem silly but nobody will see you and it is the only way of getting an accurate timing. It will also show you what facial expressions you make while you are speaking. If you discover that you always put your hand on your chin when starting a new paragraph you can make a conscious effort not to do this.

103

At the same time tape record your speech. When you play it back you can then tell whether you have any linguistic irritations to remove, such as giggling when you pause for breath or speaking too quietly.

ILLUSTRATIONS

Now that you have prepared your talk find out what you need to illustrate it. You may decide that you don't need to provide illustrations, but if you can they will improve your talk and keep the interest of the audience. But they must be relevant and clear. If you are using slides you will need to make sure that they are all properly labelled and in the right order and the right way round in their boxes. Mark your speech where each slide will be shown.

If you need diagrams or lists which are unavailable then you may need to prepare overhead projections. These can be done on personal computers nowadays on special transparent film and so the job is much easier. Do not try to put too much writing on transparencies. Your audience will not bother to read it. They want clear, easily digested diagrams, maps or a short list of points.

When you give your talk remember that you should not waste time reading what you have written on your transparency. There is nothing more irritating to the audience who can, you must assume, all read it for themselves. What you need is to expand and explain any points.

104

VISIT THE VENUE

If you are giving the talk in your own building then you may not need to visit the venue of your talk in advance. But if you do not know the place then do try to see what it is like. Make a note of any important characteristics. For example:

- is it a large hall with bad acoustics?
- is it a small room where you will be almost on top of the audience?
- is it cold, so you need to dress warmly?
- is it too hot, so you need to wear a jacket you can take off or, if the audience is formal, thin clothes underneath if you keep it on?
- is there a stage or are you speaking from ground level?
- is equipment such as microphone, slide projector, overhead projector, table, chair provided? (Don't assume any of this)

Once you have seen your venue then you can adapt your clothing and conditions accordingly.

CHECK EQUIPMENT

If equipment is being provided then check it to make sure that it is working. You don't want to find that someone has left a plug off the slide projector when you go to switch it on on the day. Make a note of any equipment that you need to bring yourself such as spare bulbs or extension lead.

PRACTISE USING THE EQUIPMENT

You may not get a chance to practise using the equipment, but if you can it will be a help. If you have never used slide or overhead projectors before then get someone to show you and spend time on your own using it until it comes naturally. You don't want to be fumbling with the equipment at a telling point in your speech. If you cannot use the actual equipment then see if similar equipment is available at your workplace and practise on that. Use the microphone if there is one so that you can pitch your voice appropriately and make sure that it works properly. You don't want off-putting squeaks from it when you start talking.

105

PRACTISE YOUR SPEECH

Ideally, of course, you should be able to practise giving your speech in the actual venue. But you are unlikely to be able to do this. Instead give the speech to your mirror, your partner, your dog, your tape-recorder and anyone else you can think of. The more you give it the more confident you will be. If you are terrified, then reading the speech word for word from your pages will be necessary. But this often sounds stilted. However, this is better than fluffing it if you feel you cannot cope otherwise.

The best option is to write the headings and subheadings only on paper or cards fastened together in the right order. Glancing at the headings will give you enough information for you to fill in the rest of the speech. Experts just put a few jokey words on small cards or give their speech without any notes at all. I don't recommend this unless you give the same speech frequently. It is all too easy to lose your place. Decide on what level of visual aid you need and keep it to hand.

DRESS APPROPRIATELY

Again you should dress to suit the occasions. Not flamboyant clothes at a staid stockbrokers' meeting or a dull suit at a presentation to local artists. Try to wear layers so that you can take off a jacket or tie or waistcoat if necessary. Bear in mind the heating of the venue and wear clothes that will keep you warm or cool enough and can be altered if the warmth changes.

106 Making the presentation

Before you start take several deep breaths to calm yourself. Everyone is nervous. You must be a bit nervous to keep on your toes. If you are too blasé the audience will become bored. Now you are in front of your audience. Your speech is prepared, your illustrations are ready and your audience is expectant. Remember, you have the winning hand unless you do something awful. Any audience starts by wishing and hoping that the talk will be interesting and that the speaker will present information well. They want you to do well.

Let your audience know at the start of the talk the rules of the game – whether they can ask questions in the middle or wait until you have finished. Bear in mind that if you allow questions as you go along, if the audience is enthusiastic you may never finish your talk!

Start off with a joke if you can. It needn't be complicated and certainly not rude. Make a joke about your work or yourself. This will warm the audience up and make them feel relaxed and sympathetic towards you. Don't overdo the humour but add it when you can. Beware of standard joke books, though, everyone uses the same jokes. If you can't think of anything, ask your colleagues.

Start confidently and speak clearly. With a microphone you should be heard at the back of the room. But if there isn't one then 'aim at the clock at the back of the room' – even if the clock is invisible! This makes you raise your head so that your voice is projected out though the room or hall. Do this even if you have a microphone but make sure that it is raised high enough to catch your voice without you bending over it. Don't be afraid of moving your hands but do not wave them about all over the place. If you stand with your arms by your sides you will look unnatural, but if you are constantly moving them they will be distracting. Occasional movement will be all right.

If you have allowed time for questions make it clear at the start how you will deal with them. 'I will take questions at the end', for instance, will let your audience know that you will not want interruptions while you are talking. Answer questions honestly. If nobody asks, which is always embarrassing, have one or two prepared yourself. You could say 'while you are thinking what to ask you might be wondering how this fits in with . . .' and then answer the question yourself. If there is still no rush to question you have at least filled the gap. End with a thank you and accept your applause!

107

PAPERS

If you are making a presentation which the audience needs to keep in mind then you may be asked to prepare a paper to be handed out beforehand or at the meeting. This should be your speech with any additional information that you will not be giving together with references and a suitable heading. If your speech is in note form this will not be acceptable for the paper, which should be written in straightforward but more formal language. Check your spelling and grammar. Your company may have a set form for papers or the organisers of a conference may have standard guidelines for the participants to follow. If so, use these. Always keep a copy of your speech and illustrations so that you can use the material again to a different audience, adapted appropriately, and for your own reference in case anybody wants to follow it up afterwards. Major conferences often produce books or reports containing the papers of the participants which is issued afterwards. In that case make sure you are sent a copy and send your paper in good time for publication.

Audience attitudes

Most of the audience will be on your side but you will occasionally get hecklers or clever-dicks who delight in trying to upset you or humiliate you.

Hecklers are not loved by the rest of the audience. A firm put-down such as, 'You are entitled to your opinion. Now the rest of the audience want to judge what I have to say', will usually be enough. If the interruption becomes abusive or physical do not hesitate to stop and ask an organiser or even some of the audience to remove the person. It is not fair to the rest of the people to allow constant interruption.

Clever-dicks are more difficult. They usually wait until question time and then ask a question which is really an excuse to give a long speech about their opinion. Learn to spot these in advance. Stop them firmly after a few minutes and before the rest of your audience gets bored: 'I'll stop you there because I want to answer the first point you raised. Now . . .'

If you feel during your talk that the whole audience is bored then you need to wake them up. If you can't think of a joke or an interesting snippet to drop into the speech then try altering the tone of your voice or using more illustrations. It may not be your fault. If the audience has already been at lectures all day or has had a late night on the town then you may not win anyway. Give your talk, cut it short if possible and put it down to experience.

A lively audience can be good or bad. It can be bad if it involves heckling or jeering. If the whole audience is against you then you must either brave it out or give up. Brave it out if you can both for your own pride and because the audience should not get way with such behaviour. Of course, if you are deliberately provoking them with controversial statements then you will be prepared for this reaction. Some people thrive on it, but don't invite it if you can't handle it.

A lively audience can be a benefit if they are enthusiastic about what you have to say. The feeling will hit you from the floor and will encourage and sustain you. This will improve the way you present the information because it will increase your enthusiasm. Your talk should be designed to encourage this enthusiasm from the start.

The chance to talk

When do you get chance to talk or make presentations to people? Consider the following possibilities:

- talk to your staff
- talk to your colleagues
- talk to your seniors
- talk to the board
- talk to staff in general
- talk to associates in other parts of the company
- talk to associates in other companies
- presentations to suppliers
- presentation to sales force
- presentation to overseas consumers, suppliers or retailers
- talk to visitors
- talk to local schools
- talk to adult education groups

There is a wide range of opportunities for giving talks. Presentations are more specialised and these are more likely to be given to people directly connected with your work. But here again you can see from the list that there are a number of opportunities for doing so.

If you have not yet been given the opportunity to make a presentation there is nothing stopping you from deciding to give one to your staff or colleagues or from asking your boss if a presentation to management on a particular aspect of your work would be informative and useful. Quite often you will find that this will be accepted with enthusiasm and your image will be improved because you will have shown initiative. Asking for time to do a presentation is good practice. First of all you can time it to suit yourself. If you need a long time to prepare then you can arrange your talk some time in advance. You may also have some choice of venue if you are giving the presentation at work. All this will give you more confidence.

Overcoming nerves

There are many good techniques for overcoming nerves. Some can be used before the day and some on the day. Use the ones that seem most useful to you.

1. **Yoga.** A good all round exercise routine and breathing control method which gives all over relaxation. This should be taught by a qualified yoga teacher. Obviously you can't get into the lotus position during your speech but doing exercises the night before will calm you.
2. **Relaxation tapes**. These contain calming music which can be played while you are awake or asleep. A lot will depend on whether you like the music or find it an irritation. Some of the same effect can be achieved by playing your own favourite music to put you in a good mood.
3. **Physical exercise**. You may not think this is relaxing but in fact the effects of strenuous swimming, running or any other sport is to wake you up and relax you. You not only feel alert but looser in body and mind. Do not try to do this half an hour before you give your talk, though, or you will be sweaty and red-faced!
4. **Massage**. This can be your partner or an expert. It is very restful as well as easing tension from muscles.
5. **Reading**. Reading something totally unconnected with your work just before you go to sleep can be very relaxing for many people.
6. **Deep breathing**. Everyone should do this just before they give their talk. It calms you down and forces you to think and not gabble.

7. **Loosening muscles**. Start by tensing then relaxing first your toes, then your legs and so on until your whole body is relaxed. This can be done anywhere and has a calming effect.

When you actually make your presentation, you can keep calm by focusing on one person at a time. Choose a friendly face about a third of the way down the hall or room and address your remarks to them. Change the person every so often, otherwise the rest of the audience will feel ignored.

Some people who wear glasses take them off so that they can see their notes but not the audience. This may be all right for a bit but the audience will be able to tell that you are not looking at them and your voice may drop and be lost if you don't keep looking up.

Alcohol is not a safe option. One glass may be okay before you start but more may make you so relaxed that you do not concentrate enough to give the talk properly. Also you are unlikely to have access to alcohol when giving presentations at work so you should not come to rely on it as a prop.

111

LEARNING POINTS CHECKLIST

1 Discover who your audience will be

2 Know your subject

3 Prepare thoroughly

4 Write your speech and practise it

5 Check the venue and equipment

6 Practise using any equipment

7 Do some calming techniques

8 Speak to the clock at the back of the room

9 Be firm with hecklers and bores

10 Remember, your audience wants you to succeed

DAY SIX ACTION PLAN

Ask to make a presentation or give a talk to your colleagues or staff. If there is no opportunity at the moment to do that ask your local secondary school if they would be interested in you giving a talk to their sixth form.

Prepare for it thoroughly by researching your subject, writing notes, writing your speech and practising it. Visit the venue to check equipment and practise with it.

Say your speech into a tape-recorder and play it back to hear any irritating faults. Keep doing this until you are happy with it. Look up some suitable jokes – try not to use well worn ones. Practise telling them to your partner – that's one way to keep your partner happy!

Try saying your speech without notes just to see how much you can remember. It will give you confidence. Prepare illustrations, by hand on transparency sheets if necessary.

Give your talk confidently and look up and speak clearly. If you are talking to that sixth form don't be patronising.

8

Handling the Press

Any organisation needs to pay particular attention to goodwill and that goodwill is largely created by the kind of publicity it gets. Organisations have no choice about how they promote themselves via the media. They all communicate with their audiences whether they like it or not. Some organisations have reputations which have evolved over the years, which may have been built by word of mouth. For other organisations the public decides by observation and discussion what reputation such companies have and so creates the reputation. Still more organisations make positive decisions about what kind of corporate personality they want and try to manipulate this via the media. With no evidence to the contrary, an organisation will be to the public what it says or shows itself to be. The same of course, can be said of individual image – you are what you say or show yourself to be. So you can adapt your image to your own situation.

So organisations are all communicating with the general public even if they do not make a positive decision to do so. It should be obvious that those organisations who particularly want to present a particular image to the public will make sure that they speak via the media.

Publicity must not be confused with advertising. Advertising is something an organisation has paid for; publicity is free. Good publicity can improve a company's image and therefore its sales almost overnight; bad publicity can have the opposite effect just as quickly. Because so much importance is attached to publicity it is obvious that someone who can present the company in a good light to the media is someone whom the organisation will cultivate. Not only will they be presenting a good image of the company to the world at large but that person's own image to the general public will also improve.

As spokespeople for the organisation present themselves in a good light, so the public's perception of them improves and by extension their perception of that person's role. A good image of that person helps the company and so the company can prosper. A person who can present an organisation in a good light keeps a high profile for themselves within and outside of the company with a consequent improvement in job prospects.

Talking to the press

The press cannot get an accurate news story about your organisation without talking to somebody connected with it. News is concerned with people and it is important that the company is prepared to let someone talk to the press, TV or radio.

Each organisation has an image which it wishes to portray to the general public. It might be efficiency, caring, speed, national distribution or any one or more of a dozen things. The personality of an organisation is shown by the attitudes it adopts and these attitudes are relayed to the public in part by the media. How the personality of an organisation is perceived by the general public can sometimes be even more important than the price of the company's product or how worthy the organisation's cause is. The success of an organisation, large or small, can hinge on how the public reacts to the firm's attitudes as portrayed in the media. Because the goodwill of the public is so important, good publicity generating goodwill is an important investment.

The press may well approach your company themselves if they are interested in some aspect of it which they think would make a good news story. In which case, they will be guided to the firm's public relations department or whoever is designated to talk to the media. It is then up to the public relations officers to decide who else in the firm needs to or should be allowed to talk to the press. Or the company may send out press releases or call a press conference if they have some particular viewpoint or news which they want the media to take notice of. In either case people will be needed within the company to face the press.

WHY IT MIGHT BE YOU

If the press want to talk to someone with a particular expertise in part of the company's workings then the company will look for someone in that area whom they can trust to talk to the press without undermining the image the company wants to put over. It could be that you are the person with that expertise and that you will be called upon to face the press. Or maybe the company has called a press conference because it wants to highlight some particular aspect of the company. You may be the best person to explain the process. So you may be facing the press.

You may be in a smaller organisation where you have been asked to handle any approach from the press, in which case you will be the public relations and press officer rolled into one. Or you may be used by the company as an example of a typical member of the organisation and be asked to represent the company image to the press. Or you may be in the news as an individual having achieved a particular success or milestone within the company. In any of these situations and many others it may well be you who is in the firing line.

Do not be afraid of taking this opportunity to promote your own image as well as that of the company. It is an ideal chance to impress not only the general public but your employers.

115

INDIVIDUAL OR CORPORATE?

If you are asked to talk to the media then you have to decide whether you are representing yourself or the company. In most situations you will be representing the company and be expected to put over the corporate image. In this case you must responsibly and consistently put forward the attitudes of the company. The public judges an organisation on the behaviour it expects to see from it. If there is a marked deviation from those expected attitudes then this causes concern.

This is not to say that you cannot project your own image and that of your own job in a good light. Simply by being prepared to talk to the press or be interviewed gives you a chance for your own personality to shine. You can do this without denying the company expectations of behaviour and attitudes. You would not be asked to represent them if they suspected that you might be going to undermine them in public.

SPECIALIST KNOWLEDGE

If you want to be the person from your company who faces the press then you must ensure that you show yourself to be someone useful to the company and who could effectively represent them.

116

To be noticed you should make sure that your day to day performance in your job is always of high quality. If you ensure that you don't skim over cracks and always present a professional image than you will come to the attention of people who matter. People who perform well always get noticed. It helps, too, to have some specialist knowledge so that you become the expert whom it is natural to call upon when that subject is discussed.

Choose an area which is undeveloped in your company and learn all about it. Ask other experts outside the company, read as much as possible in up-to-date books and articles, take training courses to keep your knowledge up to date. Let it be known that this is your speciality and offer to help other people in the company with that subject. Thus when your company needs someone to talk to the press about your subject, you will be the person they will naturally choose.

USING THE PRESS TO PROMOTE YOUR IMAGE

A company needs a defined persona and expects its representatives to present that to the press. However, different audiences must have this presented to them in different ways. The corporate message must be the same but the way it is presented can be different. For example, if your organisation prides itself on the speed of its service it may well choose to show this to clients by means of a straightforward video demonstrating the different transportation techniques. To sixth-formers this may be wrapped in a more general educational style with lots of jokes.

You will also be expected to present a team style to the press. More and more management success is achieved by team effort and a team personality emerges in management. You will be expected to present this to the press.

HOW CAN YOU STAND OUT?

You may feel daunted by this and wonder how your image can be presented if you have to toe the company line.

For a start if you want your company to recognise the importance of your job then you have to adapt your image to the sort of personality they are looking for. This does not mean hiding your natural charm, wit or exuberance (if such your personality is) but it means that you have to use these characteristics to present the company and your job.

117

If you are naturally jolly then your talks to the press may be presented with jokes while still putting forward the company line. Or if you are basically shy you may write press releases in a straightforward but informative manner – do not underestimate the relief of the press on reading a well-written and informative press release because they see so many useless ones.

Press releases

The basic way that any organisation communicates with the media, especially the press, is by use of press or news releases. These are a straightforward means of presenting information to the press. If you are the person who regularly writes them then your image is going to come through in them. Your name will go on top as the contact and the press will 'phone you for further information. If you can do this well the press will start to 'phone you as a general contact, not only about your organisation but about your special subject.

THE FIVE 'WS' OF JOURNALISM

Anyone can write a press release but most cannot write one well enough to be used by the press. The press like to have the information presented as concisely and clearly as possible. They do not like obvious publicity puffs, although these do get used if nothing else is available. Although your press release may not be used exactly as written, you should aim to write it as if it may be. As you get better at it your press releases may well be used as they stand.

Editors need to have five important facts presented to them in the first paragraph – who, what, where, when and why. It doesn't matter in what order these facts occur as long as they are there. The 'how' and any other information comes afterwards. This is because when space is short, the information is cut from the bottom so what is left at the top must tell the whole story.

118

It will also quickly tell an editor whether the information is of interest to his or her readers. If the first paragraph is of no interest then the rest of it will not get read. Yet papers and the TV and radio still receive press releases which are rambling and uninformative. If you can learn to produce a short but effective press release you will be the editor's friend.

SETTING OUT A PRESS RELEASE

If you are asked to produce a press release you may be given special company headed paper with the words 'news release' or 'press release' on it. If not, use the company paper and type the words 'news release' in capital letters underneath the heading. Although such documents are still called press releases, news release is more accurate and it means you can use it for TV and radio as well. This also shows the media that they do not need to pay for the information. Make sure the date appears so that the editor can judge how topical the information is. Also put a contact name and 'phone number (yours) at the top, so that the paper can contact you for more information or to arrange a photo.

Give your news release a title. Keep it short and informative.

It probably won't get used but will give the editor an idea of what the release is about, for example 'Lamb Fuels sponsors Maryland community festival'. Then type the information in double spacing underneath. Double spacing is necessary so that information for the printers can be written on the sheet. It is also more easily read than single spacing. Try to keep the information to one sheet but certainly not more than two A4 sheets. If you do need a second sheet type 'more' or 'mf' (more follows) at the bottom left-hand corner of the first sheet. The sheets should be numbered after the first in the top right-hand corner.

Keep to the point: 'Lamb Fuels (who) announced today (when) that they will be sponsoring Maryland community festival (what) in Northshire (where). The company hopes to encourage local people to support their local organisations (why).' Once you have written the important facts in the first paragraph you can add the 'how' and any other information. Use quotes too. Either get a quote from the relevant person, e.g. 'The Director of Lamb Fuels, Mr Charles Robinson said "We place a high value on supporting community events" '. If you are the expert then quote yourself 'Miss Emma Clown said' . . .' Anything else of interest can go in afterwards but don't waffle. Once you've said everything relevant, STOP! Then type your contact name and number again at the end on the left hand side, then underneath centre the word END in capitals. That's it.

It sounds easy but so many people get it wrong because they try to be too clever or put too much information in.

119

TIMING

There is a habit of putting embargoes on press releases to tell the editor the earliest date that they can use the information. But so many people abuse this by putting embargoes on unimportant releases that many papers simply ignore them. The only time you can put an embargo on a news release is when it would be damaging or embarrassing if the information leaked out before a certain date or time (remember the fuss when the Queen's speech was printed before it had been heard on television). If you only use embargoes on the few occasions when they are important then they are more likely to be respected. To embargo a news release type EMBARGOED UNTIL whatever date and time is necessary. So perhaps for a sensitive speech you might embargo your release until the time of the speech. On the whole, though, do not embargo anything if you can help it. This will make you seem more co-operative to the media.

News releases can be sent out at least three times for an event with slightly different emphasis: before the event will happen, when the event is just about to happen and just after it has happened. The first two are more important because that gives the papers time to write up the story and to arrange photos if necessary. The third option can sometimes be used for local papers or for something like a book publication where it is the fact of publication having happened which is important.

Your chance to shine when writing press releases comes not only in the presentation of the release and the information it contains but in how you handle follow-up calls. Make sure that you have a copy of the release to hand together with any extra information which you may be asked for. Do not rely on your memory even if you consider yourself good on the 'phone. You must be sure when talking to the press that you say what you want to say. You can ask for a conversation to be off the record but then why send out a press release? Just don't say anything you don't want the press to repeat. Have a list of other people whom the press might wish to talk to and any main points not covered in the release which might arise.

If you think that the information is urgent you can phone the paper and ask to speak to whichever reporter covers your subject. But if possible, a press release is better because you can say what you meant to say. If you do phone make sure that you have the five 'Ws' prepared and that you have all the information to hand.

Any organisation ought to be able to think of a release to send out at least once a month, possibly once a week. But be careful. Do not send out non-news. Less than once a month and you risk being overlooked. More than once a week and the press will certainly get fed up with you.

PHOTOGRAPHS

Make sure if the press ask for a photocall that you can arrange for the relevant people to be available (including yourself if necessary).

You can in your press release make a note to the editor of any photo opportunities such as:

PHOTO OPPORTUNITY: Lamb Fuels' director Mr Charles Robinson will present a giant cheque for £5000 to Maryland community festival organiser Mary Jones on Maryland recreation ground at the bandstand at 3.30 pm on Saturday July 17th.

If in doubt, put nothing. It is quite usual for an editor to make his or her own decisions about whether a photo is necessary and to phone the contact to make arrangements. If you are asked for a photograph of yourself for the media you will need to have one handy. Arrange for your company to provide you with a number of 10 × 8 inch glossy black-and-white head and shoulders photos of yourself. Otherwise arrange to have some taken professionally. Write a basic caption to be stuck on the back (do *not* write directly on the back of a photo). It should state your name, position in the company and your specialism together with your company's name and address and phone number. If the photo is to accompany press releases then mark it copyright free, so that the press can use it without payment.

121

Press briefings

These are occasions where the company calls the press and gives them an update on whatever newsworthy event the company is involved in. Because of the brief nature of the statement they are often given at short notice. They can vary from the simple issue of a brief statement to the media to a full and detailed statement by member of the company. Questions are not necessarily allowed from the media.

It is important that any such briefing contains all the relevant facts that the company wants to put over and is clear and precise. If a printed version can be prepared to hand round that is all the better. Usually someone from the company, perhaps the company solicitor, will read out the briefing statement. If you are chosen to do this it is important to speak clearly and to try not to show any emotion, particularly if the news for the company is bad. If it is good news of course, then a slight smile of pleasure may be permitted! The point is that you should be seen to be presenting the media with a straightforward, reasonably unbiased, statement. No statement issued on behalf of a company will be free of bias but a briefing should be presented as such.

If you have been told not to answer questions then the usual 'No comment' will suffice, and don't hang around after reading the statement otherwise you are fair game for questions. If you have been told you can answer questions, then make sure you have prepared the facts and are aware, by consultation with your superiors and the PR department, how far you can go in answering the questions and when to refuse to answer.

122

Press conferences

These are much larger versions of press briefings and questions are certainly allowed, even encouraged. It can involve one or more members of the organisation making statements and answering questions. While press conferences can be called at short notice, they are usually notified to the media well in advance so that the maximum number of journalists and photographers can attend.

If you are asked to participate in a press conference it is again important to know what guidelines your organisation has laid down for the occasion. Look relaxed and keep calm, particularly if the subject is a difficult one. Answer any questions directed to you as honestly as you are allowed within your brief and use the 'no comment' when necessary, but try not to avoid answering questions if you can help it as this gives an impression of something to hide. The press heckles when it is trying to dig out information so be prepared for what seems like hostility. It is not directed at you personally (unless it is you who are the subject of the conference). Deal with it firmly and with humour, if possible. Do not get agitated by it. Remaining calm under fire from the media is one of the essentials of a good press conference presenter.

Either press briefings or press conferences give you a chance to improve your image as an individual. If you are adept at handling press briefings and can remain calm while being heckled (perhaps on TV for thousands of people), then it is you people will identify with the organisation you represent. A successful début will probably mean that you are thought of again when another conference is in the offing. As a front man to a company to face the media you not only set yourself up as the 'face' of the company but as your own 'face' to the world.

Contacts

Your most important contacts will be reporters from the press especially if you are sending out news releases on a regular basis. They should be people you get to know by name and who can rely on you for accurate and up-to-date news.

Also important are local community contacts. If you are trying to promote your company locally then you need to know who can advise you of local events, local political quirks or how to get to speak to the relevant person in the local Council. Networking is encouraged here. The more people you know, the more people you will be passed on to, and the more relevant and on the ball you can make your press releases.

COMMUNITY INVOLVEMENT

Some of your news releases will be aimed at the national press, but many more will be for the local press. It is important therefore to emphasise local involvement for the local press. And when considering this do not forget the importance of the local free papers. These are delivered free to every household in an area and therefore have a greater local coverage than many of the paid for papers. Offend or ignore them at your peril.

When aiming press releases at the local press try to mention well-known local people, local events and local places. Emphasise the local nature of your organisation. Tailor each release to either the national press or to a specific area locally, depending on the coverage of your local papers. When the firm gets involved in local events make sure that your prepare a press release to reflect this.

TV and radio

Although we have talked about press releases in terms of the press do not neglect TV and radio. It depends on the nature of your organisation whether you will find it possible to get coverage in the national networks but certainly local TV and radio will welcome your news. Send out news releases to various area networks making sure that each one is geared to the particular region. A list of radio and TV stations can be found in the *Writers' and Artists' Yearbook*.

You may be asked to give or find someone to give interviews to radio and TV. These may be live or recorded or over the 'phone. Again the key is preparation. Make sure you have at least three facts that you want to put over. Then never mind what questions you are asked, steer the answers to what you want to say. Practise in front of a mirror. Pretend you have been asked questions and answer them. This may seem odd but it prepares you for the real thing. Take a few deep breaths before you go on he air. If things do seem to go wrong don't panic. Everyone will have forgotten the interview in a couple of weeks. With luck they will have remembered what it was about, which is why you should be well informed and well prepared. On TV wear something comfortable and simple and reasonably smart. Don't wave your arms about. Keep your hands relaxed in your lap. Smile!

ON THE SPOT OR OVER THE 'PHONE

If you are asked to give an interview on the 'spot, or over the 'phone, obviously you cannot be as prepared as you would like to be. But you should always have the press release and a list of relevant facts and people to hand. Take a few seconds to think before you speak and don't gabble. If you smile then the audience will hear this in your voice even if they cannot see you.

Bad news should be first news

In the worst case scenario the media gets hold of disastrous news about you and it appears in all the papers before you can do anything about it. If this happens, do not pretend it hasn't happened and do not ignore it. Get in touch with all the papers, TV and radios stations and offer to give your version of events.

Explain what has happened simply and clearly and explain what you are doing about the situation. This in itself may be enough to defuse the situation. Keep the media informed as the disaster unfolds, even if it does not show your organisation in a good light. The public distrusts organisations which they suspect are trying to hide something from them and they dislike the individuals who present this point of view. So if you tried to say nothing or excuse the event then you too would be branded in the public eyes as a charlatan. They would much rather an organisation was honest and said, for example, 'yes, we made a mess of this batch of food but we have withdrawn it all immediately, refunded purchasers and are making a new batch', rather than one which said, 'we don't know how this happened. It's nothing to do with us'.

125

If you have to present this kind of bad news, then if you are honest and straightforward you will be perceived in that way yourself. If you manage to divert the public's fury then you will certainly be seen as a useful individual to the company.

COPING WITH GOSSIP

The general principle behind telling bad news holds good for general news. Always try to supply the public and the press with as much information as possible. Lack of information results in uninformed gossip and the power of a bad word of mouth reputation to destroy a company's image should not be underestimated. As long as you supply the correct information then inaccurate gossip has less chance to breed.

YOUR IMAGE IN THE NEWS

While you are providing a service for the company you are also promoting your own image. You should be seen as a reliable source of information, especially in your own particular sphere of expertise. You should be seen as honest and straightforward. If you can also seem pleasant and approachable then you and you company are going to benefit.

What the professionals say

Colin D. Duncan. *Director of Corporate Communications, British Nuclear Fuels plc.*

I'm director of Corporate Communications, essentially responsible for deciding upon communication strategy, deciding how BNFL can communicate its business message to politicians, the media, the public and customers and doing it by formulating the messages, formulating a communications programme.

BNFL would like to be perceived as a world class professional company that can manage difficult substances like nuclear waste in a secure way. I would like to see BNFL perceived by the public as "we have this waste and if there has to be nuclear waste I can't think of anyone better than BNFL to handle it for me." We've got a good technical reputation but it's very difficult for anybody who's handling nuclear waste because it's something that nobody thinks should exist in the first place. People say there's a place in the energy industry for nuclear power and a need for nuclear power, but when you say "what do you think about nuclear waste?", they say, "we don't want it." We can't stop being human and creating waste. All we can try and do is manage waste in a way that won't damage the environment. That's what BNFL does and what I would like the company to be perceived as doing it well.

I think the way individuals in BNFL present themselves to the public does affect how the public views the company. It's a two-way thing. You can go into a room and address, say, a class of schoolchildren and if you say, "Hello, I'm from Greenpeace and I want to tell you about this" I suspect you'll get a more favourable initial reaction than "Hello, I'm from BNFL and want to tell you about this". They're conditioned to like the man from Greenpeace and not the one from BNFL. But you can overcome that initial reaction and overcoming that initial reaction comes from you as a person. If you've got a good company image it can help, but the real judgement is made upon the individuals, when you're dealing with individual people. The problem is that with a multinational company you can't possibly make personal contact with everybody so you have to rely on other tools such as the media and other public relations techniques, rather than just personal contact. But personal contact is far and away, all the research shows, the key area where you make your initial image or break your image. If it's the right person speaking to the right audience that's far more important than anything else.

I don't think there's a set of guidelines about how we should behave in public. We have a fairly extensive talks programme and we obviously train the staff and make sure they are well briefed on all the technical facts. Honesty has to be drummed into people. Don't try and make it up as you go along and don't be dishonest because you'll be found out and totally lose credibility. I would like BNFL to be viewed as a company which can be trusted to handle these nasty things. Nobody is going to trust a company who tells lies or whose staff make things up as they go along. So that has to go all the way through the culture of the company. If we're to be trusted then everybody has to be trusted and two or three people betraying that trust will make the whole company look bad.

As far as my personal image is concerned, I think professionalism has to be the key. But professionalism doesn't come from having all the answers, it comes from being able to assimilate people's views and then find a way forward to get a consensus. Often the two are confused. I view a professional as somebody who knows a bit about most of the area they're working in, doesn't have all the answers, avoids giving all the answers, because you don't get consensus, you don't get the best out of people.

I think the second part of the BNFL image is professional trust. It doesn't mean to say BNFL has to be arrogant. Technical arrogance is often something that people accuse the nuclear industry of having and that comes from "we're professional, we know best". We won't do that. BNFL's been knocked off its perch by all sorts of both market forces and by anti-nuclear groups. Competition destroys that kind of technical arrogance. We're going to have to become more customer-oriented and BNFL has become incredibly more so in the past 10 years.

We make more personal contact with the public and the customers. We show more willingness to listen, to be open, responsive to new ideas, and to negotiate to be more customer friendly. We've shown to the outside world that you have to be listening, you have to be willing to adapt what you might see as the right way forward because the people disagree with you. You have to learn to do that within a company as well. If somebody wants to say I'm wrong on an individual level, I'll listen and I won't hold it against them. I might still decide to do what I've decided to do. I might decide to change my mind. Changing your mind isn't a sign of weakness.

128

The values we want to communicate is the outside world have to be the values that we communicate internally. I communicate those values in my everyday work with my staff who can begin to communicate those values to the outside world. Then people will be able to trust us, rely upon us, and see that we are professionals and we've got the confidence to say, "maybe we'll rethink that point". Most companies which have persistently ignored what the outside world is telling them have gone out of business.

I don't like my staff to be arrogant. At the same time I don't like them not to express views openly. Some of the best views come from heresy and I don't think consistency is a prerequisite of professionalism. I think consistency is the product of a mediocre mind, to be honest. If everything has to be consistent then that assumes the world is consistent. I think we have to accept things are not going to be like that and that each judgement has to be made on the basis of the facts alone.

It's been said, "it's not what you look at, it's what you see that's important". You may have a brilliant person but if all you see is a shambling idiot then you really have to think very carefully about what you're going to do with that person. You don't expose him to customers or the public because by doing that you're not being fair on them. All the customers will probably see is a shambling idiot. So image is highly important.

It's often said in BNFL, "why do they say this about us, it's not the way it is", when the media are being particularly unfair. But the way it is is the way people see it. If people see you as threatening the environment, killing people, then that's the reality and we have to change it. The way to change that reality is to change that perception. So if somebody portrays an image of a shambling idiot, that's the reality. They may be brilliant underneath but unless you can harness that brilliance in some way it's certainly not going to be very helpful to use them as a company representative. They are just portraying an image that we do not want to portray.

I think the thing that's helped me progress more than anything is involving other people and not thinking I have all the answers. Some of my worst mistakes have been avoided by other people saying "well, hang on a minute, maybe you shouldn't do it that way, you should do it this way". It's this openness that's important, so your staff are not scared to disagree with you. You still might decide to walk into a minefield but then it's a decision which is made fully and you're totally responsible for it.

It may be a team decision but the responsibility is still with me. You cannot say "we all made this decision therefore we're all to blame". I think that's a cop-out in a management position. "We all made this decision and if it goes wrong we'll still learn to live with it but I'm the boss and I'm to blame", that's the way it should be. But you'll find if people believe you're serious when you say that, they will move heaven and earth to avoid that decision backfiring on you so you very rarely have to take the responsibility because it goes very rarely completely wrong. It could be a bad decision but they'll make a bad decision work because it's a joint effort. Whereas if you make a bad decision on your own, people will work to make it fail because they don't feel bound. You have to show that you're willing to back your staff when things get tough. It gives messages to people that you're willing to go in and fight for them. You've got to mutually support each other, especially when it's a difficult exposed area such as public relations in the nuclear industry where everybody's looking for you to make a mistake.

Ten years ago we picked people to meet the public on their technical ability. Now it's more on their communication skills, personality, their interpersonal skills, and their technical ability's secondary. This is even more important if you're doing TV or radio interviews. We're drawing up a central list of people who are good communicators, no matter where they work, office services or the nuclear physics department, and those people will be the people we can rely upon to do most of our communication. We've got a writing competition on at the moment in the house journal where people are invited to send in articles and we'll give prizes. We're also running television training and radio interview courses and public speaking courses and those people that shine on those will go on the list. They're doing it for personal improvement but we're trying to get a list of our good communicators. It doesn't matter if they know everything they need to know about how a nuclear reactor works. What is important is that they can communicate to the public that a nuclear reactor is safe. We have completely put out of our head this idea of putting the technical expertise person on the air or in front of the audience.

We don't say, you've got to look like this. The key thing is to keep the best of that person, which is normally the bits that cannot be learnt and you can't ask people to unlearn things. You can give people tips but you can't create a new person. If you try to do that they come over as false and of course we're looking at trust. What our public are looking for is genuine people who are genuine communicators and if they're genuine they'll trust them. If they're too well rehearsed, then they won't. There's that fine line between being professional and being slick and if you're not careful you train people to be slick.

When you say "image" to people they think it's dishonest. As I said before it's not what you look at, it's what you see, and that's the key. In my view there is no such thing as reality or fact, this is the way it is. Anything is open to debate, so everything is open to be viewed in a number of different ways. Projecting an image is not projecting something which is dishonest, you're simply putting a point of view. For every point of view there's a counter point of view, so when you talk about a company's image it's never fixed for ever. It's changing, it's evolving, and will change and evolve as society demands change. You have to listen constantly to what society expects, and then manage the company to respond to those expectations. That doesn't mean just having an image, we must actually have most things going on within the company. If they aren't we'd be found out in five minutes and the image would be destroyed. So image is not a gloss over the reality; it has to be reality.

LEARNING POINTS CHECKLIST

1 Keep up to date with your work
2 Make yourself known to your PR department
3 Become a specialist in an aspect of your work
4 Learn to write a straightforward press release
5 Remember the five 'Ws' of journalism
6 Have some photos of yourself prepared
7 Prepare for press conferences or briefings with your PR department
8 When giving a briefing answer questions honestly
9 Do not get fazed by hecklers
10 Keep up to date with media contacts

131

DAY SEVEN ACTION PLAN

You can start by making a list of all media which might have an interest in your organisation. Include local papers and the trade press. Use *Willings Press Guide*, *Benns Media Directory* or BRAD (*British Rate and Data*) to help you. Check for the names of editors in the *Writers' and Artists' Yearbook* or the *Writers' Handbook* or phone the switchboard and ask.

Arrange to have some black-and-white photos taken either by the company or privately.

Practise setting out a press release. Look in your local paper for a piece of news and then try and write it again as a press release, remembering the five 'Ws' of journalism – who, what, where, when and why.

Buy an address book or keep a special section in your Filofax or on your palmtop computer to note the name, number and organisation of reporters you get to speak to personally. Ask to sit in on the next press briefing to get experience of how it is done. Make notes of how the speakers dealt with difficult questions and hecklers.

9

Events

You not only have to present yourself to your colleagues, staff and boss at your place of work. Your image is something which must be seen to be carried out of the office. You need to make the most of any opportunity to represent your employers.

Why should that improve your image and worth in the eyes of those who can affect your working future? For a start, it shows enthusiasm for your work. If you are prepared to go out and tell other people about it or at least show your face on occasions when your firm is being represented, then this shows you are keen. It also shows a pride and confidence not only in your own work but in your employers. If you are prepared to stand up as representative of your company, then you are in effect saying 'I approve of what my company does and I have confidence in them to deliver a quality product or service'. The fact that you show willingness to be present on the occasions when your company is showing itself to the outside world will enhance your image as someone who wants to go far in the company and who can represent it well.

There are many occasions when you can take the opportunity to present yourself to the outside world. Some of these occasions may seem to you to be boring or unnecessary but they will give you a chance to show yourself and be seen by the rest of industry or people in power as well as engaging the attention of your immediate employers. This chapter will tell you about some of those occasions and tell you how to make the best of them and yourself.

Exhibitions

There are a number of occasions when your company can take a stand at an exhibition. These can range from the enormous trade fairs at venues such as Olympia to small local affairs in the town hall. Whatever the size of the venue your company will no doubt think itself wise to be represented. If the rest of your industry is there then it will be conspicuous by its absence. 'Are they afraid to compete?' will be the thought behind everyone's query about its absence. In the same way, while your absence will go unremarked by other people in your area of work unless you are well known, you will not get to be well known unless you are prepared to show your face at such places.

We are not talking here about the two or three people who stand and hand out literature at the company stall or who demonstrate one of the products, although that has its place. Often these can be people hired for the occasions with no knowledge of the job you or your employers do. No, we are talking about the person who answers the visitors' questions, who can tell them exactly what the company policy is, who will be going round and talking to other company representatives and to the media if they show up. In other words being the company for the occasion. There may be one or several of you to do the job but you all have the same basic role: to show your company in the best possible light to anyone who wants to see it.

Sometimes the exhibitions are only for the rest of your industry, in which case you are showing what the company can do against the best of similar trades. But customers will still be there. Sometimes it is open to the general public. At all times the media can show an interest. From your point of view you are there to show not only your loyalty to the company but your own ability and to raise your profile. You cannot know at any outside event whether that person from a rival company who seemed impressed by you will be your new employer in a few years' time.

What will impress people is how well you can explain the company. It does not impress anyone who asks a searching question (and sometimes the simplest questions can hide a serious point) to be handed some literature and dismissed.

When people ask questions at stands at exhibitions they want answers from someone who is not going to dismiss them as silly.

The actual setting up of the exhibition stand will not be your responsibility unless it is part of your job to organise staff. However it is as well to be prepared for what it will show. Check out the following:

- how large will the stall be? One table, several, a roomful?
- what literature about the company or job will be available?
- will there be any products or services being demonstrated?
- will there be a visual aids display, perhaps in an adjoining area or room?
- is the company running any kind of competition?
- how many demonstrators and assistants will there be?
- will any senior members of the company be present at any time? Will they be available to talk to the public?
- will you or any other senior members of the company be giving a talk? If so, how often and where?
- will you be assigned to the stall or can you wander about and talk to other people?

Once you have an idea of what is involved you can work out what your role will be.

Of course exhibitions are not always a stall or counter. They can be screens of pictures, a display of models on stands or indeed anything which will stimulate and interest people. You need to decide with your staff how much and what you can say to people. You don't want to be saying cheerfully to everyone 'Yes, we are going into major production on this product' when the company wishes to tell people in six months' time that it will be going into production. It could result in a lot of frustrated customers!

Again, as with all public representation, preparation the key to success. Remember that you will be on show not only to your own company, but to the rest of the industry or profession and the general public. Make sure that you find out all the things you didn't know about the company. If there is anything in the media which is not favourable and is likely to prompt sharp questioning from the public them make sure you are properly briefed on the subject and can make straightforward replies. Evasiveness will not go down well.

Dress smartly and wear a name badge. You want people to remember you! Have your own business cards to hand out to interested people as well as general company cards.

Conferences

We have already in the previous chapter discussed presentations and talks where you have the opportunity to talk to an audience. But often you will be invited or sent to conferences as a member of the audience.

Sometimes conferences do seem a waste of time; the chance, many people think, for travelling to a nice place, eating and drinking a lot and turning up for the occasional lecture or discussion. Obviously, you can treat conferences like that. But if you return to work with little positive result from them then you have wasted your own and your employer's time and are not likely to be sent on one again. Look on the eating, drinking and sightseeing as a bonus if it is provided but concentrate on getting the most out of a conference.

Start by reading any literature or conference papers you have been sent. This will give you an idea of the theme of the conference and what topics will be covered. Some may not be relevant, in which case you can legitimately skip those. But be careful. If you dismiss everything as not strictly relevant to your present situation then you may be losing the chance to absorb new ideas or thinking. One of the jobs of a conference goer is to take back new perspectives on company policy.

Make sure that you are taking any papers that would be helpful. Although as a member of the audience you will not be talking yourself, it may be that people you speak to afterwards have an interest in what your work involves or what your company is doing and it is useful to have some information to give them. Your business cards should be used to the full.

HARASSMENT

Women on their own sometimes find conferences difficult because they are not taken seriously or some of the male participants try to make unwanted advances to them on the grounds that anyone at a conference is there for a good time and is fair game.

It should go without saying that any man who tries this is not doing his image any good at all. He will be, or should be, despised by both male and female conference participants for this kind of behaviour. In this day and age it is sad that one should need to remind men to be chivalrous but if you see a woman being pestered then you should go to her rescue. It is difficult enough for women on these occasions without having to deal with unwanted male pests. Women should be taken seriously and treated with respect as should all participants.

136

BE A JOINER

Much of use at conferences goes on outside conference time itself, at the bar, over dinner or at events laid on by the organisers. You also have a chance to meet people from related areas of work, senior people, and people from outside the industry who have useful things to tell you.

To take advantage of this extracurricular information you have to be a joiner. It does not mean that you have to go around being the life and soul of the party but you need to make an effort to mix. This can be difficult for naturally shy people but simple small talk and a willingness to listen will take you a long way.

LISTENING – THE VITAL SOCIAL SKILL

In fact, the ability to listen will win you more friends and arguably be of more use than the ability to tell jokes and be the centre of attention. Try to spot the conference bore but listen to what other people have to say. A few well-chosen remarks to encourage the speaker will make you popular. You can learn a lot from other people at conferences but don't think you will remember it all the next day, especially if you have been enjoying a drink or two.

When you get back to your room make notes of anything of use from the lectures themselves and the people you met. Many seasoned conference goers dictate useful thoughts into a tape-recorder for transcription later. Make notes on your conference programme too. Don't assume you'll get given a free biro; turn up with your own and a notebook.

Open days

Here your image is on display to the world and his dog. Anyone who wants to turn up on an open day should see you and your organisation at its best. However, your best must be on view all the time!

Although companies like to have open days and say 'take us as you find us – we're always like this', in fact, a lot of preparation has to go on. You can't have the public wandering into dangerous or sensitive areas or going unescorted into a heavily populated area of work and causing disruption. Somebody has to show them around and interest them and explain to them what is going on.

You can have senior members of staff doing this and many like to do so especially where small numbers are involved. It gives them a chance to meet their customers and show the company in its best light. You can do this too. If you volunteer or are asked to show people round on open days do not disparage it. You will be fronting the company to the public. It is your image that is on show and it is you the boss will remember as the person who dealt so well with the public.

Ceremonial functions

You may not be lord mayor but you may well have to attend ceremonial functions on behalf of your profession, job or company. These can be such things as opening branches of your shops, presenting awards to people in your industry or making speeches at formal dinners.

In all these cases you are not only representing your company but your profession or job. You are the shoe industry, the accounting profession or the garden equipment retail business. Dress smartly and make jokes but remember that for the participants this is an important occasion in which they play the starring role. Your job is to act as facilitator between them and their instant of fame.

Retirements

If you are asked to turn up to someone's retirement do, then you must do so if possible. Even if you do not know the person involved very well you represent the future of his or her profession and as such are an important reminder of their own time in the company.

You may as a senior manager be asked to make the presentation or give the retirement present. This can be a tricky moment. Do try to find out some details about the retiring person. Like funerals, the moment can be flattened by banal generalisations spoken by someone who clearly barely knew the person concerned. If the partner of the person retiring is there do try to make them feel welcome. For many it will be their first and only time in their partner's place of work, meeting the people their partner has known for years but who have only been names to them.

Try to make sure that the gift is appropriate. Even if there is a standard gift from the company such as a gold watch or clock (heaven help us!) then try to have a collection and give something more personal. Consult the family to find out what the participant would really like. A colleague will usually do this anyway but it does no harm to enquire or gently initiate such an idea.

Some people are well known for their view that 'I don't want any fuss when I retire. No presents, definitely'. In that case you have to judge whether they really mean it or are simply nervous that no one will care when they go, anyway. If in doubt, you can give a quiet gift to the family of something neutral but useful, such as book or record tokens, which can be shared by everyone.

Make sure that there is transport provided for the participants if they are not driving themselves. If they are emotional either from sadness or drink then they should not be driving themselves home.

There may also be a party for a move to a new job. Here the problems are similar but not entirely the same. In this case if the job move is for promotion then it may seem silly for people to give a gift. But certainly a party or other social occasion is acceptable.

WHAT IF IT'S YOU?

An important point here: when you are the recipient of such attentions, whether because of retirement (not yet!) or moving to a new job then you must not embarrass people by disparaging their efforts on your behalf. If they give you a present open it in front of them and exclaim with pleasure. People want to see that you liked what they chose for you. If you don't open it at once they will either think you don't like it or that you have already been told what is in it.

139

Have a few words prepared – just a few will be adequate but make them heartfelt. Talk to everybody, especially the secretaries who will have done much to organise the occasion.

Anniversaries

Every organisation has anniversaries – even a year in a new company can be celebrated. They are excuses to praise the firm's product and service, emphasise history and tradition and raise the firm's profile in the community. You too can be part of that image making process. If nobody seems willing to organise a celebration you can suggest it. Perhaps a donation to a local charity formed at the same time, articles in the press or the production of an anniversary book. If there is to be such a book why don't you offer to write it with the help of the company archivist? By simply suggesting this you will have shown that you have your company's interests at heart.

Christmas

In some ways Christmas can be very trying for a manager. You want to get on with your work but at the same time you do not want to be seen as a killjoy. If you do not join in to some extent then your image with your staff and colleagues could be damaged because they will consider you humourless and unsympathetic.

If you are senior enough then it is possible to take your team out for a meal. Your secretary can arrange the details and will have more idea than you of the sort of place everyone will enjoy. Make sure that everyone is invited, that is, secretaries, clerks, assistants and so on. This is an occasion when all ranks of staff should get together.

You will be expected to be convivial and join in the humour. Do not feel you have to make a complete fool of yourself. Some dignity is expected from senior staff but if it amuses everyone to see you wear a Father Christmas hat, it will not do any harm! Be careful how much you drink. You want to be careful not to commit any indiscretion when drunk but make sure you allow your team to drink what they like and arrange for taxis home. A common solution is for everyone to pay for their own meal while the manager pays for the drink – so start saving up now! While you should not over-indulge in alcohol make sure that you are careful to forget any behaviour by staff which is out of character or over-reacting, unless it is unpleasant or dangerous. Christmas dinner is not the time to criticise behaviour.

Other Christmas events include concerts or shows. If you can join in with these, so much the better. The manager who plays the piano for the Christmas concert or the person who sings a solo in the company choir will be remembered by colleagues and bosses alike. Your image can only be improved by showing ability and willingness to participate in such pleasant company events.

Dinners

While Christmas dinners are a special case, formal dinners have their own purpose. They can be huge affairs where people from related trades from all over the world come, or smaller one-table affairs when business is discussed by colleagues and seniors.

Dress is important. Read the invitation carefully. Dress is still defined by what the men should wear. Lounge suits means a smart work suit in a dark colour with the ladies in a smart dress which can be any length. Black tie means dinner jacket for men and smart short or long dress for ladies, usually slightly dressier than normal wear. White tie means tails and a white bow tie for men and the full-length evening gown for women.

The usual etiquette rules apply. Sit where you are placed or where your name card is and seat the ladies first. Use your cutlery from the outside in or watch what everyone else does. Good manners dictate that no one will comment on any *faux pas* you make so don't get in a panic if you think you've used the wrong knife. Most people are so unused to formal dinners that they won't know anyway. No smoking until the end of the meal when someone will announce that you can do so. When in doubt don't. Smoking is often considered bad form nowadays.

Address conversation to your neighbours on your right and left in equal measure. Try to find something in common. For big formal dinners which are for show rather than business it is small talk which is needed. Women often find these occasions trying because they do not know anyone and have not even business in common, so try to find topics of mutual interest.

For less formal dinners where the aim is to discuss business you should dress formally according to the invitation but you can, indeed are expected to, discuss business. That does not mean that the whole evening should be devoted to work but that is the aim. Often, unfortunately, such dinners can be only for men. If you find this is the case then you should be wondering why there are no women in senior positions in your company or what other reason there has been for excluding them.

141

Seminars

At these you are expected to make a contribution by preparing a paper for discussion. You will either be expected to read it out at the time or prepare it for distribution beforehand. Make sure it keeps to the point and that it is in keeping with the theme of the seminar. If necessary, discuss your choice of subject with the organisers beforehand.

Trade fairs

Like exhibitions these involve meeting the public and the rest of industry. You are showing your competitors and suppliers what you can do. You are presenting an image of the company which will be a marker for the rest of your profession or industry. 'We need to match WRT firm's quality of production'. You, yourself, are the front man or woman for your company. If you can explain or present your product well, then you will form an impression that the rest of your industry colleagues will remember. When it comes to head-hunting time it is the person whose name brings a picture of recognition that will get the first offer.

142

Professional societies

It is important for your image to attend meetings and events of your professional or trade society. Not only is it important that you keep up with the latest news and work practices of your job which the society will provide, but you will gain stature and impress people, by getting your face known in the profession. If you can, take office or edit the magazine or in some way become a permanent part of that organisation. That way you become one of the people everyone thinks of when they think of a particular profession. The media will come to you to ask questions about your work, and your boss will consider that you have some extra edge on knowledge about it.

Trade unions can act in a similar way. But in that case a lot will depend on how confrontational your union is, or you are, with the management. If you are put in a negotiating or confrontational position with your senior staff it can act against you. On the other hand, if you handle it well and fairly, it may even do you good if you impress with your organisational and negotiation skills.

Secondment

Some people avoid secondment because they fear that being away from their original job will mean that they lose in terms of promotion and recognition. In fact, nowadays, secondment is seen as a necessary step for advancement in many careers. Take the chance for secondment if offered. Not only will it broaden your outlook but you will learn new skills and be able to bring this back to your original job. Far from delaying your promotion it is more likely to hasten it, as you will have more to offer than those who stay behind.

143

You can keep up with what has been going on at base by having regular meetings with colleagues and attending meetings and dinners where invited. Talking to friends over a drink after work can be enough to keep you in touch with the ins and outs of office politics.

What the professionals say

Chris Casburn. Manager, Corporate Image and Direct Marketing, Mercury Communications Ltd.

My job is part of a central function which is called Marketing Services and exists to co-ordinate the activity of marketing communications throughout the whole of this company. Our role is to ensure that the company focuses the strength of the people in our three distinct business units and also gets the best value for money from the activity. My particular area of coverage is direct marketing – design of literature, corporate identity, sales promotion, conferencing and audio visual. We

have a set of brand values which we try to ensure that everything we produce adheres to. This is to focus on the customer, to
question the traditional. That's very much part of the image
side. So we're young, we're dynamic, we're thrusting, we're
forging ahead, we're leading – all those sorts of ideas.

We have tracking studies which evaluate people's perceptions of us and the feedback certainly is one of welcoming
the David, in the sense of David and Goliath. There's this new
entity that's come into being that is challenging the old ways.
So we have a very large groundswell of support from Joe Public
who want us to succeed.

I think we have an overall philosophy of being easy to do
business with and being very open. We've had a very involved
programme of employee attitude surveys, where they've asked
the employees, 'what do you feel about the company, what do
you feel are the strengths and weaknesses?', and then fed that
back and openly given out the answers, to say, 'look, here we
are, warts and all'. So I feel that the openness is vital to the
philosophy of Mercury, that if you've got something to say you
should say it. Approachable and easy to do business with is very
fundamental to the way we wish to be perceived.

I think individualism and entrepreneurial flair are
encouraged. Being smartly dressed and appropriate to their
audience would be the way most of the sales force would
approach their customers. It would of course depend on
whether they were approaching a Japanese bank in the City, or
another customer in Edinburgh. We have a series of territorial
marketing teams, so I think it's very much designed to be
receptive and focus on individual needs throughout the
country. The individual approach has to allow for flexibility. We
do strive to have a consistent identity programme: for instance,
all our slides and overheads and brochures work to a specific
design grid, which means that if there is a manager presenting
from Scotland joined by somebody from head office and a
colleague in sales, the presentation stuff will be consistent.

I think my strengths are to question the traditional way of
looking at things; to say, 'well, just because that's how other
companies have done it, do we really want to do it that way?' I
think my creative edge is something that I really feel is able to

144

be developed here and it gives me a lot of excitement working for Mercury. I think the ability to make quick decisions, to be able to say, 'there's an opportunity, let's be decisive', and without six levels of bureaucracy above having to filter it out is also exciting. So I try to be creative, decisive, quick-thinking, and the company responds to people who wish to be that.

I think the route to Mercury has probably allowed some of my strengths that were identified in the interviewing process to shine more here than in other companies I've been in. So I would guess people who look at me now would probably see me as able to be more creative, do more things, again questioning the traditional, stretching the horizons, being first, which previously I probably felt I mumbled on about but were cut off in their early days.

I think the only important thing is to recognise that in certain circumstances one would expect, depending on the audience, to present a more formal image, less enthusiastic, move my hands around less. But I think I suffer changes really, rather than real personality change. I must say take me or leave me!

145

My weaknesses are that sometimes I find it difficult when other people don't quite see the wavelength I'm on. Perhaps I'm working on something that I see as being a real opportunity to shine and be different and there are perhaps people in more traditional roles, dare I say it, the accountants and engineers, who say, 'yes, but it's never been done that way before'. I would say certainly, compared to previous companies I've been in, that here that element of entrepreneurial flair is encouraged to survive. I think again it's very much why the business was refocused into business units so there are clear business areas to go for and develop the strategies that each of the units need.

When I talk about corporate image, that's the other side of the work I do. I'm very aware that we produced three volumes of a corporate identity manual and that it doesn't stop there. It is every time somebody answers the 'phone, the way, even out of work, you bump into someone in the pub and how eager and keen those people are to talk about the company and the way they will do it reflects the corporate image.

We in this central unit of marketing services have a specialist unit responsible for conferences and events, and also an area responsible for corporate hospitality, sponsorship and so on. We all share those ideas and adhere to the same brand values to ensure that everything we do is reflected in the same light, be it anything from a major conference of 500 people, to a small conference of 10 or 15. We do try to ensure that we've got the same quality there, that we've got the same openness, the same creative edge, an innovative leading edge in whatever level we work, from the design of our stands upwards. At the big annual conference for telecom managers our stand was evaluated by independent research and came out as the most exciting, the most visually stimulating stand on the day. So we would hope that that would carry through into the advertising (which has won golden and silver awards in its category for business to business advertising) through to the literature.

We try wherever possible to use account managers on the events and exhibitions, as they really are the people that are the experts in meeting the public. So we don't bring in merchandising teams, but use the skills that we have. Usually we'll have training first. So in the major events a lady who works for me rehearses anybody doing a presentation to either an external or an internal audience. She will go through the scripts with the speakers, rehearse them, make suggestions where necessary, tactfully say 'That's a bit rambling, a bit long, those slides don't work with 27 bullet points on'. So we have a central resource. It's in my area, in fact, to help people with that. Certainly presentation skills I think are an important item. Within Mercury training courses are available for that and it's certainly something that people are encouraged to go on up to management or indeed supervisor level, as well as courses in negotiating skills and other growing areas.

You have an appraisal of the last year which identifies where you met your objectives and also identifies what skills you need to develop, so that if you're out meeting people you clearly need presentation skills, negotiating skills. There's also a development plan, which means people look ahead 3–5 years and which might say, 'okay, you're corporate image and direct marketing manager now, Chris, but if you really want to become the general manager of one of the business units you need to develop these additional skills of, perhaps, greater financial awareness,' and then we have a programme built in to build those up.

We again usually use feedback forms and we do presentations, particularly presentations at our own internal sales conference. So where each of the speakers from the chairman through to marketing directors of various business units spoke we would get feedback and evaluation from the audience so we would be able to say to them all, it seems this bit was a bit over their head or it wasn't particularly appropriate for that particular audience on that day. I'm not aware of anybody standing up at a public forum and people going 'wow'. I've presented the awards along with the judge at the direct response innovations awards and I've also spoken at the direct marketing conference. Obviously it's business marketing. There wouldn't be a switch of image, I think.

We haven't adopted an image policy or image training. Again we would, in terms of presenting conferences or seminars, either internally or externally, have a resource here to say, 'you really need to be less technical in your presentation, you need to actually look around more, involve members of the audience, you need to slow it down, you need to cut out the slides, you need to hear what you're saying'. So we advise people on how they present to people.

I think individualism is really quite encouraged. I think it would be a very 'unMercury' thing if everybody was the same and regimented. It's not a bank-like atmosphere as I'm aware and I've worked for some of the national institutions. It's an open and energetic atmosphere where the odd explosions occur from time to time. They're quite applauded, I think, as long as they're controlled. I think inevitably they will occur and I think the series of training courses that the company runs is helpful – it's about dealing with conflict, it's about dealing with managing change and so on. It's when things are changing quickly that conflict points arise. Having programmes in place acknowledges that managers need to be able to be trained on how to cope with those shifts in the company. But people are aware that there will be conflicts and try to understand how other people see things and encouraging internal communication to

147

say, 'I understand your point of view, but . . .'

I could certainly say that most people think a company's image or identity is linked to focusing on the logo and I think one of the key things that we do here is to realise it's much wider than that. From the way we answer the telephone anywhere in the company, to the way that somebody off duty on the golf course or in the pub would present the company and talk about it and how knowledgeable they would be about discussing what's happening. So I think in terms of the people image it's probably fundamental to the recruitment policy. I would hope that they certainly have an idea of how they want to see Mercury growing and I would hope that they are looking for individuals with flair and expertise and innovation that really want to break barriers. So I'm sure it starts at that level and there is a distinct type appearing in Mercury which is mostly young with a lot to say and who are not too frightened to say it.

148

'Mercury in the UK' is a 36 or so page document which explains what we do, how we fit in within the regulatory system and the structure of the business. All the images are of Mercury personnel. We believe that in this brochure and indeed any others we should use people in real situations. We encourage our staff therefore to be involved in that, and all the images are of Mercury people in real situations. None of these are studio shots. They are all shot in and around the building.

The corporate video which we've just produced again sets out to use Mercury people in real situations talking about the company. So it has one of our engineers, and two account managers who again are not actors hired for the day. It is very much on policy to use our people talking about our service, with no actors involved at all.

LEARNING POINTS CHECKLIST

1 Your presence at company events will raise your image
2 Use conferences to bring back information
3 Single women at conferences should be treated as valued colleagues
4 Take part in company events

5 Why not suggest an anniversary celebration?

6 Don't be afraid to lose your dignity at Christmas dinners

7 Make retirement parties a positive experience

8 Formal dinners can be fun but don't worry if you get things wrong

9 Take an active role in your professional society

10 Don't refuse a secondment

DAY EIGHT ACTION PLAN

You should now be taking stock of opportunities to make your presence felt to the general public and the rest of your industry. Make a list of all possible occasions – use your diary to help you. Make a note of all occasions you could take part in. Are there any you could volunteer for? Which will you be expected to attend anyway? Start saving for your staff Christmas dinner now. Buy a Father Christmas hat! List everyone who should be invited.

If you are not a member of your professional association or society find out what it is and contact them to arrange for membership. Make a note in your diary of when the next meeting is and attend. Volunteer for any job you can reasonably expect to do well.

Find out what you can about your company's history. Are there any obvious anniversary dates coming up? If so make a list of possible anniversary celebrations to present to your boss. List activities you could be involved in. Is there a company history? If not, suggest that you co-operate in writing one.

10

Community commitment

I f people relate to you as an individual then they will think more kindly of your profession or company. But you do not meet all your clients or potential customers in the course of your work. The only way to meet more of the general public is to take part in some of the many community activities and projects that every area has.

It would be easy to become cynical about this area of image-making. Why not join in local activities simply to promote your business? Because people are not fools. If you are not interested in or not concerned with what you are participating in, people will know. That will detract from your image just as much as taking a genuine part will enhance it.

You should be taking part in your community life for your own sake. If you have no interest in anything the community has to offer, how can you expect to go into work with a lively and interested approach to life? And on a practical level, how can you have an understanding of people's needs if you restrict yourself to business life? Becoming involved in community affairs keeps your feet on the ground and enables you to put back something into the community which supports you and your business.

People like people

Very few individuals go, or should go, out into the community and start to advertise their job. That will only put people off. More rewarding is to work quietly but enthusiastically on a local project and for people to appreciate you for your own efforts. If they should then later, in the course of conversation, discover what you do for a living then their opinion of you will be enhanced. At the back of their mind will always be then 'X company, oh, yes, isn't that where that nice Miss Y works who does our charity accounts so well?'. The personal satisfaction of doing something well for other people on a voluntary basis or contributing to a local project in a simple way will make you feel more confident about yourself as well as contributing in a positive way to the world around you.

How do I start?

If you have never consciously looked around your local community and wondered what it is you can do for it, then you may well be surprised at the number of different opportunities on offer. This could range from joining a local political party, helping with a charity, becoming involved in your religious community activities, to helping at a school fete or editing the local campaign's newsletter. The choice is endless.

151

To start, ask yourself what issues you really care about. What help do you want to give the community? Are you interested in, for example:

- the local hospital
- politics
- charity work
- your religious community
- children
- those with physical difficulties
- those with mental difficulties
- ethnic minorities/equal opportunities
- women's issues
- local schools or colleges
- the elderly
- local amenities and environment
- local traffic problems

- local history
- national issues on a local level, e.g. CND, Friends of the Earth?

When you have decided on what interests you then ask at your local library for a list of local organisations which are concerned with your areas of interest. Then contact the secretaries of these groups about how you can join, when the next meeting is, what you can do to help. Many local organisations have a lot of members but only a handful of people who are actually willing to do something practical on a regular basis. If you offer practical help and make a firm commitment you will be welcomed with open arms.

CRACKING THE CLIQUE

When you start going to meetings of local groups you will sometimes find that there is a well-established clique of people who, while they may pay lip service to your offer of help, may in fact try to keep you out of things. This is a form of fright. They have not the confidence in their own powers to allow anyone to help them. They are afraid that they will be ousted and become valueless.

This is the time to use tact. Offer to assist Mr Z with the accounts, bow to his expertise and do not tell him he is doing it all wrong. In time you will end up doing more of it 'so you can learn' and although it will still be 'Mr Z's job' other people in the group will be well aware of who is doing the actual work. Or try a different tack and offer to do the one job that *nobody* wants to do (there always seems to be one). It may not be glamorous or exactly what you want but it will get you accepted into the clique and keep you in with what the group is doing. You can then take the opportunity to do other things as time goes on.

KEEP OUT OF INFIGHTING

Do not take sides in personal disputes in any local community groups. All it will do is alienate the rest of the group from you. Keep neutral, keep busy and keep smiling.

Community jobs on offer

There are a number of voluntary jobs in the local community for which your employer, if you are not self-employed, must give you time off during work to do. These include being a school governor, being a JP, or being a local authority councillor. Most companies are good about allowing people who do these jobs time off, but others do not honour the law or may make things very difficult. Approach your employer directly and be prepared to negotiate for a reasonable amount of time off to do the job. After all, it will be in his interest for you to do this. If you are a JP or a councillor you will get limited allowances but certainly not enough to make up any lost wages or salary.

If you are a self-employed person then you can decide for yourself how much time you will devote to the job. Bear in mind that these jobs have a minimum attendance regulation when you are expected to be there; for example, as a school governor you need to attend a minimum of one meeting each term. If this is during working hours then you must make every effort to attend them. Here are details about a number of community jobs which are well worth doing.

153

SCHOOL GOVERNOR

School governors are needed now as never before. The introduction of local management in schools and the problems caused by the National Curriculum mean that governors have a very busy and active role to play. What they decide will have a real influence on the way education is delivered in their school.

Even if you have no children of your own, or none at the school where there are governor vacancies, do not be put off applying. If you do have children at a school where vacancies on the governing body occur you can put yourself forward for election through the school. Your local Education Authority has a duty to ensure that every parent or guardian of a child in the school is informed of any governor vacancy and forthcoming election for school governor. If you are a teacher at a school you can ask to take part in any election for teacher governor vacancies.

If you are a member of a political party you can ask your ward to keep you on their list of nominees for LEA-appointed governors. These are appointed by the local council on recommendations from local political parties. If you are a regular church attender you may be able to become a Foundation governor of a local voluntary school. Foundation governors are chosen to make sure that the school is run according to its Trust deeds. However, you may feel that your politics or your religion should be kept out of education, especially if you do not want your business to be seen as slanted in a particular way. You may prefer to become a co-opted governor.

The other way of becoming a school governor is to be co-opted on to the committee. In fact you may do well to try this way as governing bodies in LEA-maintained schools are advised to co-opt governors from among those people who are not normally represented on the committee, such as local business people and ethnic groups. Write to the education department of your local council or to the Chair of the governors of the school and ask to be considered for co-option. To remain as a governor for your term of office, which is four years, you must turn up at a minimum of one meeting each term. But any conscientious governor will want and need to make visits to the school and attend staff selection and other meetings and attend school events. Getting to know the school and its problems is a large part of the governor's job.

It is hard work and you will find that a lot of your time is taken up with reading information sent to you in great quantities from the council, the government, the school, etc. Learn to skim but *don't* be one of those awful people who turns up at governors' meeting saying, 'can we postpone this discussion? I haven't had time to read this document yet'. Make the time or you will waste everyone else's. Above all bear in mind that, whatever anyone else may telly you, the school should be run well for the benefit of the *children*.

On the plus side, the school is one of the hearts of any local community. You will not only meet teachers, governors and council officials, you will also meet the parents, children, their friends and relatives and other local people concerned with the well-being of the children.

154

CHARITIES

Charities can range from the local hospital, the 'save the cats' charity, to local offshoots of national charities such as Mencap or CND. Whatever your interests you will be able to find a charity which needs your help. Helping is not confined to standing around on a street corner rattling a tin (although nobody is going to refuse your help if you can do that!). Charities may need help with visiting people, talking to local groups, help with accounts, editing newsletters, sticking on stamps or delivering leaflets. Even making the tea has a place to play in keeping things going!

You don't have to wear a T-shirt saying 'XYZ firm supports NMK charity' to give your image a boost, the image in this case being one of caring and concern. Simply the fact that you are there helping will do the trick. But it is especially important in a charity not to do it for the sake of your image. An elderly person or a small child, for example, is not going to be fooled by an insincere helper or bored assistant. You must do it because you really care.

155

BE THE EXPERT

If you want to help a local group but are uncertain what you could offer take a look at what skills you already have. Are you an accountant or do you deal with finances in a general way in a big company? If so, why not offer to do the books? Are you an expert on PR, a writer of exciting company reports, or a computer expert? Why not offer to edit, write for, or print the newsletter? Are you a skilled speaker at company presentations? Why not offer to give talks about the group to local people?

The trick is to offer yourself as an expert. Small groups cannot afford to pay professionals large sums to do things like keep and audit the accounts, produce the newsletter or obtain publicity. Nor can they pay for one-off help with, for example, surveying a local building or preparing for a legal battle. So if you have professional expertise be generous in offering it – free, naturally. This may seem to be too much like what you are doing already. But doing something for the fun of it and for the community good will not seem at all the same thing as producing the same work under the everyday pressure of your job.

KICK OFF WITH A SPORT

If voluntary work is not for you, then you may find that you can become involved in the community on other levels. One way is to take part in local sporting activities. This not only gets you in touch with local people but with people from other communities if you play against 'outside' teams or individuals. The socialising aspect of such occasions should not be underestimated. Your skill at badminton or as half back may be as useful in improving your image as your portrayal of being 'a jolly good sport'.

156

THE BEST OF THE REST

Sports, charity work and campaigns are not the only way to be involved in community affairs. What about joining in any local leisure groups or classes such as art, dancing or archaeology? Are there any social groups which you would like to belong to such as the Rotary Club, British Legion, WI? All have their uses. People who have a regular religious commitment may feel able to extend this by taking part in the many social and charitable causes supported by their place of worship.

Sponsorship

Sponsorship is another matter altogether. In this case you may or may not expect your company's name to be mentioned in connection with the activity or charity or campaign. But money changes hands. It could be a case of turning out for your team in an 'XYZ company T-shirt' or by donating a sum to the local hospital. Publicity is involved and the company's name gets mentioned. How you handle this will depend on what you want to achieve. You should be very careful about being involved in any sponsorship activity which is foolish or dangerous or will encourage unsocial or dangerous activity in others. Responsible firms will not ask this of their members and will not look kindly on members who involve themselves in such activities.

Take care that any sponsorship is for an activity which is worthwhile in itself, preferably one which you care about and which you would have contributed to, anyway. You do not need to be so crude as to wear the company T-shirt but just accept gracefully any publicity which does accrue to you and your business.

If you hand out money indiscriminately and expect a lot of publicity in return you will improve neither your image – nor that of the firm. You will simply be seen as a publicity grabber and your commitment to the activity will be suspect. You will have reversed any good which might have come from the sponsorship.

157

GOOD THINGS AND BAD

It should go without saying that in your private life you should not take part in anything which would discredit you or your firm or that you will feel ashamed of. Most people will not do that anyway and some will resent the implication that their business should dictate how they live their life.

But think carefully. Would you trust a car hire firm where the managers were frequently stopped for speeding? Would you send your children to a playgroup where the organisers were organising a campaign against opening a local nursery school? Unfair as it may seem, people will judge you by what you do outside office hours.

If you decide to involve yourself in something dangerous, offensive, illegal or just plain stupid then people will think of you like that. And if they think of you in that way, that will reflect on your profession or firm. There is all the difference in the world in the public's mind between being a whiz on the speedway circuits and joy-riding round an estate on a Saturday night. One is seen as dangerous but well-organised and respectable, the other as illegal, dangerous to others and unpleasant.

What the professionals say

Barry S. Hyman. *Head of Corporate Affairs for Marks and Spencer plc*

I look after media and public relations matters and publications; in addition I also look after community affairs, customer services and the company archives.

This company portrays an image of a company which espouses some very simple and fundamental principles: they are to provide top quality merchandise at the best possible value in comfortable stores, using all the tools of customer care which are available to us. We also like to be thought of, and indeed evidence suggests that we are thought of, as a company that pays back into the community in which it trades, because we spend something like £6 million a year on our community affairs programme.

By and large the relationships with the community, with the general public, the shareholders, our suppliers, the City, are on the whole good and – it sounds terribly immodest but it's a fact – we're extremely well thought of for being not only an efficient company but a company that has honest values.

I don't know that we instil in anybody a philosophy of having to portray an image, but when you come into the business you get an immediate set of principles drummed into you and indeed unless you imbibe them you're not going to be any part of the organisation. They involve not only becoming professional at your job, but also caring enough about it to want to train other people: not to hold information closely to your own chest and deny it to others, but also to be prepared to talk openly to outside audiences about it. I don't mean a formal scenario. But if people ask, be prepared to say what the company does. So I don't know that there is training to carry the image forward but it happens by virtue of the way that people are treated that they go out and boast about their company. They're proud to work for it and they talk about it and get well received.

We have a large community affairs budget and while a lot of that is donated and decided upon centrally by my Community

Affairs Department, a proportion of it is given to stores, and indeed each store has a budget of its own to use locally. They are encouraged to take on projects in the area which might be of interest to them and to look at donating money to them.

They do it in a variety of ways. They might give as little as £20 or £25 to the local school sale or they might decide on something bigger. In addition to that, the stores also fund-raise. There is a great sense of community in most stores. The majority of them always have a project on. If they decide to fund-raise for a given project – assuming we approve of the project, and of the way they're raising the money (and we won't sponsor dangerous sports) – then we'd like them to do that. We have a matching fund scheme centrally so if any money's raised we'll match them from the central pond. But the stores do a lot locally and even when we decide to give money centrally we will usually, if we can, do it via a store.

So if a hospital or an educational establishment or a prison reform group, or whatever, writes to us, we will say to the local store, 'what do you know about them?' And if the store says, 'I wouldn't touch them with a barge pole' the chances are that we won't. Or if they say 'there's no reason why you shouldn't' or 'yes, you certainly should', then we'll go ahead and investigate them properly and make a commitment. And when the cheque is handed over we usually get the local store to do it. Very often the store then takes an interest in the charity after that.

We give encouragement to anybody who wants to do work as a school governor or as a JP. We do our best to make sure that a reasonable amount of time off is given for them to fulfil those civic functions. Clearly if everybody was a school governor, a JP, or mayor for a year, we would have problems. But as it doesn't get to be anything significant, by and large, we encourage people to take part and we facilitate their doing it. I personally am involved in the local trust in the village where I live. I work with my own synagogue, a variety of things. So I've always espoused community involvement.

We don't do much commercial sponsorship. Now, if we do get some nice publicity for charitable things we do we don't say "no". But they're not done on the basis of seeking publicity, they're done because they're the right things to do in the

159

circumstances. We do not eschew the benefits which come from it but certainly individuals are not asked to go out and seek publicity for the company.

We take a lot of notice of what the public say. I do customer services and we get 3000 letters a week. It sounds like a lot but when you consider there are 12 million customers a week it's actually not a lot. Most of those are simply, 'I bought this, it doesn't fit' or, 'it's got a fault, can I have my money back or an exchange' or whatever. But you do get suggestions, and pictures emerge. Six years ago we introduced changing rooms. We didn't have changing rooms before that. But you then got to a time when people were busier and the pressures came on for a changing facility. So we put them into stores and now all the major stores have changing rooms. So that was a response.

The store staff are our main ambassadors, sales assistants, and they're doing it all the time every day. Every time there's a transaction, and they look at you and smile and say 'thank you' they're enhancing the image of the company. If they look down and ignore you and stick the change in your hand while they're talking to their friend you go away with not a good impression of Marks and Spencer. So clearly there is training going on in customer care in stores all the time. If we get a complaint about an individual in a store then I would speak to the store manager. All cases will be dealt with on an individual basis because there are often two sides to a story. But if a customer's gone away unhappy that's no good to us, whatever the reason. So our objective when I get a complaint is to say, 'the customer is an ambassador for us'.

We are not a business that spends a lot of time going around conferences. On the odd occasions when we do these things it tends to be the media relations and corporate affairs group who'll go and represent the business. If it's finance it would tend to be one of the finance professionals. But other than that it would tend to be us, the generalists who amass over the years an encyclopaedic knowledge of the business, who go and talk about it. I think we try and be the same thing to everybody. Now clearly, if you're in a formal environment talking to groups of people, you pitch what you're saying to your audience. To try and tailor it would effectively be patronising and I don't think we want to try and do that. We try and pick the right message for the right audience but I don't see that we perceive a need to tell a different story to different people.

I think when you're talking to professional audiences, the financial analysts, the journalists, they will not be in any way 'wowed' by your sweet talking them; they won't be remotely impressed. They're looking through you at what you're saying. When you go into social groups who are just there for a nice pleasant evening, to learn 101 things you never thought you wanted to know about Marks and Spencer, yes, I think they look at you and say, 'gosh, what a nice chap that must be. Marks and Spencer must be a nice place if he works there'. So to that extent the message they receive is different even if you don't set out to give different messages.

In head office when we're sending people out to talk we don't say, 'now, make sure you've got a smart suit on, and smile', or, 'brush your teeth and talk politely; stand up to speak'. Those things come and somehow or other the people who do those things are the people who have the aptitude for it. You find that those who haven't don't do it and you don't press them to anyway.

It's different at the top. I try to persuade my Board of Directors that speaking to the media and doing it well is now a part of their job and I help to get them training for it. M & S runs a series of training schemes through your career which you can opt to go on, but it doesn't take people who aren't on my side of the business and say, 'You need some media training because you might be on telly one day'. I make sure that the people in my area who do deal with the media take PR courses and training so they are equipped to do the job.

I don't think image pushes you forward or holds you back, in all honesty. Clearly, you have to have a social acceptability in a company to progress. So, taking on board that your behaviour is reasonably conventional and that it fits within the framework of a big company in which you have on many occasions to subordinate your own will to the will of the majority, then I don't think your individual personal style necessarily advances or retards you.

What will decide that is your talent at the job you are given to

161

do and the appraisal you get at the end of the year for having been a merchandise manager or a food technologist or a refrigeration expert or a press officer. People will look at how well you have done that job and they may well say, 'he's very prickly but he does that job extremely well; we can make allowances because he represents the company well'. I don't think, say for the caveats I put in, that personal image counts for an awful lot. Nor should it, it should be ability to do the job and deliver.

Master your brief, know the detail, be able to control your area, manage your people and do that effectively, give them loyalty and guidance and leadership, but let them get on with the job and make mistakes and take the blame for them and don't disassociate yourself from and don't worry too much about your own personal image. I have at times been told over the years that I was either too flippant or too serious. Well, that tells me that people are making snap judgements and that really didn't matter in the end.

162

In this company I don't think that individual image is the make or break factor in your career planning. I think really you have to understand the needs to fit into a larger society and if you can't do that – if you are an individualist or an entre-preneur who cannot readily accept the discipline in team decision making or team responsibility – then you ought not to stay because you won't fit in well. You'll have a team meeting and you may not agree with what is said, but at the end of the day you had your view expressed, you've had it listened to, the decision doesn't go your way, you've then got to go for Cabinet responsibility: 'okay, so that's what the team wants, that's what we'll do'. If you can't handle that you should go because you'll live a frustrated life.

You can be a bit of an individualist, you can have an offbeat sense of humour, you can wear a beard if you like, you don't have to wear white shirts and navy suits. So people are pre-pared to see the odd idiosyncrasy and certainly I can think of at least one board member who is very idiosyncratic in his style, his mind-set and his capacity to be very offbeat and off the wall, so it doesn't hold against you.

There are disciplines in any big organisation which you need to follow but I don't think you need to be a company man or woman in the sense of just wearing a grey suit. You can be your own personality. But as long as you're prepared to accept the disciplines in a big business which it needs to have to get the work of the day done then you'll progress. I think there is always a degree of luck in being in the right place at the right time and a degree of nepotism in any business, I suppose, but that aside, by and large you will progress in the main on your ability to do the job.

LEARNING POINTS CHECKLIST

1 Being involved with your local community will enrich your life as well as improve your image
2 Choose an community activity in which you are genuinely interested
3 Be tactful with cliques
4 Consider established community jobs such as school governor or JP
5 Keep out of infighting
6 If you get involved with a charity be prepared to help regularly
7 Use your expertise to get a volunteer job with a local project
8 Do not take part in anything dangerous or unpleasant
9 Be careful how you use sponsorship
10 Local sports can spread your image outside your immediate community

163

DAY NINE ACTION PLAN

Make a list of all the skills you have to offer. Don't just think of obvious skills but be broad in your list, e.g. can you offer:

1 Designing
2 Press work
3 Writing
4 Building skills
5 Bookkeeping
6 Advertising skills

7 Team management

8 Events organisation

Make a list of your interests. Contact your local library to find out what local groups there are which match your interests. Write or phone to offer your skills.

11

Image extras

Everyone out there is projecting an image and trying to impress. What will ensure that you will be the one to impress the customer, catch the eye of the boss or be considered for head-hunting by a rival firm? What will make you stand out? It doesn't have to be anything as unsubtle as wearing a bright spotty cravat or an outlandish hat. It needn't even be something about the way you look; it can be something about the way you behave, the way you speak or how you spend your time.

When you have made that good first impression it is going to be the little things that count, that make you stand out from the crowd. Polished shoes perhaps, if other people don't bother to keep theirs in order; a smart folder if everyone else is using broken cardboard files; time spent in a worthwhile hobby that gets known to others. You can't tell exactly what it is that will encourage people to look more kindly on you but you can be sure that little things will put people off. They may warm to your personality and style but be put off by a scruffy watchstrap that they only notice a week later when they next call. Your image has to stand the test all the time. This chapter will tell you about some ways in which you can keep ahead of the image game. It will tell you about some of the things which are overlooked by other people and which will win you points in the image game.

Free time or fertile time?

Obviously you cannot spend all your free time in activity, however worthwhile. You need to eat, sleep and spend time doing useless but enjoyable things. This is not only for your health but your sanity. If you do not indulge yourself on occasions and get an adequate amount of refreshment and rest you will be in no fit state to do your job well, let alone spend extra time on image improvement.

But you will undoubtedly have some free time in which you have nothing particularly useful to do. (If you are spending *all* your waking hours at home catching up on work then you need extra helpers or a better organised day). You may think that nobody is going to care what you do in your spare time but you will be wrong. It does come to people's notice if you are doing something useful or worthwhile with your spare time. It does not necessarily have to be charity work or community work. Why not learn a language? It may not be necessary in your job now but it might be soon. It will keep your mind active and be fun as well as useful. You may be aware that you need to communicate with the rest of Europe now but have you done anything about it?

What about taking a course which will help you keep up in your subject or profession? Not necessarily a course for your job but a related course. Another area of art history for a picture restorer? Financial management for a middle manager? Why not offer to run a local club? You will not only be doing something worthwhile for your community, getting to know people, but will gain valuable managerial experience or financial practice in an informal environment. At the very least you should be doing something that uses your brain. And here I do not exclude the practical creative subjects. As any artist will tell you the intelligence and concentration needed to produce a good picture or piece of craft work is equal to studying a more cerebral subject such as maths.

Keep fit, too. A new generation of people are growing up without the regular physical activity that our forebears knew. Swimming, cycling, a team game, aerobics, for example, will all keep you fit as well as increase your adrenalin and leave you relaxed.

Where does image fit into this? Someone who has a worthwhile and satisfying way of using their leisure time is also someone who has an enthusiastic and forward-looking attitude to things, something interesting to talk about other than his or her job. That enthusiasm and pleasure in life will rub off on everyone you meet. If your activity is also practically useful to you in your career then that is a bonus.

NO NEWS MAKES A BORING PERSON

If you only read the newspaper for information about your job or the cartoons then you are doing yourself a disservice. You may be brilliant at what you do, but if you have no intelligent comment on the world at large or enough interest outside you work to make interesting small talk, then you will not be projecting an image of someone who is on top of things. It may be wonderful to be a computer expert and to spend your life reading computer magazines but that way you run the risk of being labelled as a computer bore.

Remember that your image follows you to whatever situation you find yourself in. If you have to attend business lunches and have no intelligent small talk word will soon get around that contact with you is best kept to the minimum and about business only. While business lunches are intended to further business in more relaxed surroundings, they are also a means of furthering business friendships and for making an impression on useful associates. Few people keep strictly to business discussion. There is always a need for a little lighter conversation. If you have not kept up with the news then all you will have to discuss is business and that will make for tiring if not tiresome conversation.

Make it a habit to read one of the major newspapers from cover to cover every day and one of the Sundays. Not only is it pleasurable, relaxing and keeps your mind working but it will keep you up to date on a variety of subjects outside your own sphere. The day of the scientist who couldn't discuss art or the designer who knew nothing about electricity should have gone by now. Your image needs to show a whole person, one who can relate and empathise with any number of people. By reading the newspapers you are gaining insight into a variety of views and opinions which will make your own more informed and intelligent.

167

ARTICLES AND REVIEWS

It does not occur to many people that to improve your image you have to get yourself known. This does not mean that you have to become famous overnight. But it will do your image no harm at all if your name appears in magazines, newspapers or on the radio as an expert on something.

Do not back off in horror and say, 'but I'm not an expert on anything'. You certainly are. You are an expert on your job at whatever level it is. If not, you should be if you have followed the advice in Chapter Four and have concentrated on studying one particular area of your subject. In any case a you can talk about your own particular situation.

LET'S TALK LETTERS

One of the best ways to start getting your name in the press is to write letters on your professional subject to newspapers, magazines, trade papers – indeed any publication which has a letters page. To keep your name in front of your colleagues you should consider writing to the trade papers covering your area and the specialist papers on your subject. Do not despise the in house magazine either.

But be careful. You may want to impress by writing long, verbose letters. This will not do. Letters to any publication should be kept as short as possible to put your point of view. They should keep to the facts, be written in a clear style and be as short as you can make it. This has two advantages. First of all a short letter is much more likely to get published than a very long one. Publishers are always short of space and on a letters page they like to get in as many letters as possible. The second advantage is that readers will get through the letter and your sound point on the subject to your name a lot quickly than if they had to plough through a whole page of extraneous words. A sharp well-written letter with your name and title at the bottom (e.g. Marge Thomas, Financial Director of ABC Company) will stick in the readers' minds. With a long letter you may risk the reader getting bored halfway through and turning the page. The chance to get your name and views noticed will have been lost.

REVIEWS

As you become better known you may be able to offer yourself to the editor as an expert reviewer, that is someone who can review books on one particular subject. This is particularly possible if you are an expert in something abstruse or highly technical which would be beyond the capabilities of a general reviewer.

An editor may put you on a 'reviewers' list' and contact you if any suitable book comes up. Otherwise you could suggest a book to the editor for review in a specialist magazine. As you are the expert you will be the person most likely to have a copy of the latest work on that subject. Reviewers can get guidelines about setting out a review from the magazine.

ARTICLES

You can try writing articles on your speciality or interest for suitable papers or magazines. Study the length and style from a recent copy, type your article double-spaced and send it to an editor. In your brief covering letter don't forget to mention your qualification for writing the article (e.g. I am Senior Computer Programmer for XYZ Enterprises). If you are accepted, do not press for payment. Your aim is to keep your name in front of people in your business and to establish yourself as an expert. Later, if the editor asks you for an article then you can discover whether they will be willing to pay. Once you have had a few articles accepted you may find you get your photo in the magazine. That too will help to make your name stick in people's minds. As an expert with public exposure you may find that reporters will 'phone you up for expert comment or to talk on the radio. All of this raises your profile in the minds of your colleagues, superiors and the general public.

Do not limit yourself just to writing about your job. If you have expertise in something else – perhaps you are a sales manager who is an expert on antique firearms or an insurance agent who knows about orienteering – then you can write about those 'other' things that you do.

Newsletters

You may decide that you need to keep in contact with your department by issuing your own departmental newsletter. This can be as simple as an A4 sheet printed on both sides or as complicated as a 16-page glossy document. With desktop publishing and/or the resources of a large organisation it should be possible to produce a monthly departmental newsletter of reasonable quality.

The advantage of producing your own newsletter, of course, is that it gives you a chance to put your own style and viewpoint over within the company at regular intervals. Subject to the usual rules of common sense, legal problems and your PR department, you can say what you like, how you like. Involve as many of your staff as possible – show what your department can do. Although it may only be for departmental distribution your newsletter will have a wider range than that. Copies will be taken home, passed to friends in other departments, ideas will be borrowed by the PR department, senior management will expect to see copies. You will get known to a much wider audience.

170

HOUSE JOURNAL

I have already mentioned the house journal or magazine as a place where you can try to place letters and articles. Do read it. In it you will glean a lot about the company you work for and what goes on at different levels within it. You will get a glimpse of the concerns of other people within the organisation and get to recognise people by their photos and letters. A good house journal should not simply be full of pictures of the chairman. If it is, try and get that changed by suggesting branching out.

CUTTINGS

When you do appear in print try to get a copy of the article, letter, photo or whatever. Or a tape of any radio programme you appeared in. This is not just for your personal vanity (okay, it is a bit!). Besides building your confidence by showing that you *can* do it (I did it once, I can do it again), it gives you a collection of PR information which you can use to further your writing.

You can use what you have written in a letter to write an article or vice versa. In some areas a portfolio of cuttings to show clients or superiors can make a difference to how you are viewed. It is also important to have the information to hand so that if a reporter says to you, 'you said in your article that ...' you can see exactly what you said and make an informed comment upon it.

Business paperware

This covers a wide range of paper and cardboard that you use every day in your business. Remembering that it is the small everyday things that impress after the initial image has been measured, you should take care of the details.

But beware. If you go over the top in designing business cards or fax sheets you will simply look naff. You should aim for something classy but slightly understated, something which says, 'I know I am good but I don't have to shout loudly about it'. While a flash letterhead may impress some people for a short while, it will grate on people over a long period of time. You need your stationery to say 'this is classy, this is capable, this is trustworthy'. You will not do this by overdoing the design work. Your letterhead needs to have certain obvious information on it:

- company name
- company address
- company telephone number/fax number/telex number
- VAT number
- chairman's name/director's name

In a large organisation you will get issued with letterheads, envelopes, compliment slips, business cards and all the other paraphernalia of business paperware.

In most companies it is usual to be issued with paperware

personalised by the addition or substitution of your own name, title and contact numbers below the company letterhead. However, this will not always be the case. What can you do to personalise your company ware? You may have a chance to alter the design slightly if you can put in an order.

But one of the best ways of personalising your paperware is by the way you have your name printed on it and how you sign off your letters. For example, you may have your full name printed rather than Mr/Mrs/Miss/Ms or just initials, so you would be Johnny Bank rather than Mr J Bank or J Bank. You may sign off as 'sincerely yours' rather than 'yours sincerely' or add 'with best wishes' or even just put 'yours'. All of these make a difference to how the recipient views you. How you sign your name can affect your image. Do you use a fountain pen or a biro? Black ink or green? Don't underestimate the power of the colour in which your name is written. And don't forget that for some reason those crazy letters that all organisations seem to get at some time or other all seem to be written in green ink, so that colour in a signature may not produce a favourable reaction.

172

Do you sign in an unintelligible scrawl (which annoys many people even if your name is printed beneath) or a clear hand? Consider how it looks to others. How you sign off is important. Some people are always the more formal J R Bank, others are always Johnny Bank. How do you want to be known? Do you want to be seen as approachable or more formal in your everyday dealings?

Simply whether you have the greeting typed or write it in yourself makes a difference. One senior civil servant always writes the 'Dear Samantha' in by hand – a subtle but instantly recognisable way of implying that individual attention has been given to the recipient. The slight extra effort this entails is worth a great deal in how well he is viewed. If your company goes in for lurid design and coloured paper try to find out whether you could omit the more garish and unnecessary part of the design and have plain white paper. Even just changing to white paper of a suitable weight will tone down the over-florid effect of some company letterheads. Paper should be of a reasonably heavy weight. Very thin paper gives an illusion of cheapness and suggests that the company is not doing well and this reflects on you. Conversely your image will suffer if the company insists that your letters go out on cheap paper.

BUSINESS CARDS

Most people overlook business cards as an image tool or are unsure how to use them. Your business card should be kept uncluttered but contain all the necessary information. Your name and title should be sufficiently clear and well placed that the recipient does not have to search for it. The company details should not overwhelm the card but be sufficiently clear so that they can be easily read. The company logo likewise, while an obvious recognition symbol, should not take over the whole card to the detriment of the basic information. It *can* be left off without people failing to find your company. Again how your name appears on the card can affect your image. If you want to personalise it further, take the time to sign a few and store them for handing out.

One person I know went on a business trip abroad with his name and company details typed on pieces of paper because he had run out of business cards. Never be in that position. It does not impress people, even if your image is perfect in other respects, if you cannot reciprocate the basic courtesies of business life with the exchange of clear and durable business cards.

Contrary to many people's belief, business cards are useful. Many business people store them and although they may not immediately make use of the information, may call you or your company much later. If your information is to hand they will be more likely to call your company than to ask their secretary to spend time searching the 'phone book for a company whose staff they have never met.

Not only does a good business card advertise your business without you having to say a word but it acts as an introduction to strangers in the business world. A card presented tells them enough about you to start a conversation and to give them some idea of your position in your company. The mere fact that you have a card says that you consider your services professional enough to put into permanent form. But a cheap card will

173

undermine this image so make sure your card is well-designed.

A word about size. Ask for your card to be standard size. If it isn't it would be worth your while paying for it to be printed on a suitable size card yourself. There is a tendency nowadays to go in for large cards. These look like, and often are, tradesmen's cards, and while they have their uses are difficult to fit into a wallet or purse, and also they cannot be stored in standard business card storage files. A card approximately 8.5cm × 5.5cm is adequate. Also do not make your card too small or the information will be lost. The design, it may be obvious to say, should be landscape rather than portrait. The business card is normally held with the longest sides horizontal (landscape). If you print your writing the other way it means that it has to be turned to be read and will merely irritate the recipient. In the same way it will not be easily read when stored in a wallet or card wallet file. And if it is awkward for people to use it is less likely to be read.

174

Be lavish with the distribution of your cards. You cannot tell how or when someone will make use of the information on it. Personalise it further for particular people by writing your home number on the back.

Personal contacts

Do not eschew personal contacts. Networking is not a new concept but one which you would be foolish to ignore. Obviously you should not simply choose your friends and acquaintances by how they can be useful to you or how knowing them could enhance your new image. This could easily backfire in any case as company and inter-company politics change the factions.

Instead get to know people of similar interests and expertise. Do not be afraid of asking their advice and be sure to return the favour by giving a helping hand when you can. The fact that you can 'phone up 'Bill' or 'Mary' in XYZ Company for advice gives you more chance of getting the information you want than phoning 'Mr W Black' as a comparative stranger. Keep a note of personal details that crop up in conversation so that you can say 'Hello, Bill, nice to hear from you. How did the children enjoy camp?' before getting down to business. It oils the wheels and creates a personal bond.

Having said that, you should not simply choose your friends and acquaintances for what good they can do you. It does not need a lot of intelligence to understand that hanging around with people who would be considered by most people to be unpleasant and untrustworthy does say something about you. You may have a perfectly good reason for cultivating such people but most other people are not going to understand why. They will judge you by what they see and hear of your friends. It may be unfair, but then again why do you want to know such people? Think carefully about it.

WORK SOCIAL LIFE

One senior manager of my acquaintance always turns up for the staff Christmas party or Christmas meal out, even though it is really only enjoyed by the junior staff. He feels it is important to get to know all his staff as individuals so that he knows the secretaries as Sally and Bob and not simply as Mr Dale or Miss Jones' secretaries.

175

It also shows staff that you take their interests seriously. There are occasions such as leaving parties or other office social events where the talk is of work and there is a chance to meet people from other companies or other areas in your own company on an informal basis. If you do not turn up you may be viewed as stand-offish or having an over-inflated sense of your own importance. If you do attend be careful not to drink too much or behave in any unsociable way. It is a useful opportunity to broaden your circle of friends and acquaintances.

See what other social activities your company offers. Is there a choir, a sports club, a poetry circle? Find at least one thing to take part in if you can. Apart from enjoyment it is a way of meeting people from your company. Certainly, playing the piano to accompany the singers at the staff Christmas concert will get you noticed by the chairman! Such notice may well come to mind if he or she meets you or hears your name spoken later. Very useful as long as they enjoyed the show!

Some people overdo the office social round to the detriment of outside activities and their home life. A partner or children may not take kindly to being excluded and only seeing you briefly during the week. A happy home life of whatever kind is important for your well-being and the well-being of those you care about and who care about you. If you do not make an effort to look after your loved ones, what does that say about you?

LEARNING POINTS CHECKLIST

1 Don't ignore the details; other people *do* notice

2 Use your spare time wisely, some of it for worthwhile activity

3 Try writing letters, articles and reviews

4 Take an interest in the house journal

5 Consider starting a departmental newsletter

6 Keep your business paperware clear and uncluttered

7 Don't ignore the value of personal contacts

8 Keep cuttings of your published work

9 Contribute to work social life

10 Don't ignore your home life

DAY 10 ACTION PLAN

Now is the time to take stock of those little things which many people overlook that contribute to your overall image.

Start with your social life and acquaintances. Go through your diary and see how much spare time you have after work. Decide on an activity which you would find fulfilling and pencil in some time which you could devote to it without damaging your work or your family life. Leave some 'nothing to do' space for total relaxation. If you find it difficult to relax consider learning yoga or a relaxation technique.

When you have decided what you want to do, write a list of people you could contact to find out about it and do so as soon as you can – perhaps during one lunch-time or evening. Then *do* it. Find out when the first meeting or activity is that you can go to and ink it in your diary – do not let anything deter you. Make sure that you choose a time and activity which you can be committed to. Only going three times doesn't count.

Make a list of subjects which you could write on with confidence.

Include outside interests as well as work expertise. Then make a list of all the trade, specialist and other magazines and newspapers you could write to. Start straightaway by writing a letter to your house journal on a relevant subject. Keep it short and clear, type it and post it. Star one subject to write a 500-word article on and pencil in time to write it and submit it during the week. Pencil in a regular time to do some writing. Obtain a cuttings book and decide to fill it by the end of the year.

Consider starting your own departmental newsletter. Make a list of all the people in the company whom you would need to talk to and what you would want to see in it. Pencil in a time to talk to at least two of these people the next day.

Get copies of all your office stationery. Lay it all out on a table and consider how you could personalise your paperware. Make an appointment with the company design team to discuss changes or consider having your own printed. Collect examples of other paperware which you consider effective from other companies and compare them to your own.

Look through your diary and see how many work social events you are attending during the next month. Too many and you won't get any work done. None, and you are not getting to know people. Ask your secretary to get you a calendar of company social events and decide which one to go to and pencil it in your diary.

177

Talk to your family and decide how much time they can spare you for without feeling neglected. See if there is some company activity to which they would be welcome. Pencil it in.

Long-term plans

You may have spent time and effort on improving your image. But unless you make an effort to maintain it your image will simply fade away in people's minds. Being an overnight wonder may bring you to the attention of the world but will not help your long-term prospects in your job. This chapter will tell you how to keep your image untarnished and how to make sure that you keep in the public eye in a way which will ensure that your image is presented at its best.

The better part

> Reputation! Reputation! Reputation! O, I have lost the immortal part of myself, and what remains is bestial.
>
> Cassio in *Othello*. Act 2, Scene 3, line 254

Your reputation in your job is what will determine your future career and how the general public and your colleagues rate the work you do. It is what will ensure that your work is valued and that you are valued for the work you do. As Cassio and many before and after him have found out, a good reputation is hard won and easily lost. As a vital part of your total image it is important to maintain a good reputation. This will involve work on your part but you cannot afford to ignore it. The one month when you let your image slip is going to be the one month when your clients need that vital order and take their service elsewhere.

Regular review

You cannot be sure that your image is as good as it should be unless you take time to review it at regular intervals. Do not just think, 'I'm doing OK. Work's fine and people seem to respect it.' If you don't keep up the effort you may lose that respect next week. Ask yourself these questions once a month:

1 Is my work up to standard? How can I improve it?
2 Are my customers happy? How can I improve my service to them?
3 Am I being as involved as I can be in work and social activities?
4 Am I giving as much as I can to my colleagues, staff and boss? How can I improve my relations with them and involve them more in my work?
5 Am I dressed appropriately for my work and for work-related occasions?
6 Do I need any training in any particular subjects?
7 Are there any events I can volunteer for?

179

These are the kind of questions you should be asking yourself regularly. Unless you constantly review the situation you are in danger of letting your image slip.

Be positive

It would be easy to think that you are not making any progress in improving your image. If whenever you review it you only think of where you have gone wrong, you will not be encouraged and you will neglect your image even more. When you review it think of the ways in which you have improved it. They need only be small ways but making a note of them will inspire you to greater things. For example have you in the past month:

- spoken to a member of staff you don't usually speak to
- given a talk to colleagues
- changed an aspect of your clothing
- learnt something new about your work
- joined a voluntary group
- suggested an improvement to customer service

JOB PROSPECTS IN MIND

Your image may have improved but have your job prospects? If you have been following this book and you have kept an eye on future needs they should have done. It is no good just thinking for today. Keep an eye on what the company or your job area will need in the future. If you can see that there will be a call for financial skills in a year's time with company expansion then now is the time to take training so that you are well placed to take advantage of improved prospects.

Looking ahead does not just involve learning new skills. It could be that management is being changed and that the company is looking for a new type of person. If they are now looking for go-getters with ideas rather than sound but dull administrators now is the time to improve your communication skills and present ideas to your boss. This also applies if you are looking for jobs outside your immediate area of work or workplace.

180

Make the changes on time

Obviously it is no good waiting until the last minute to make the changes that will improve people's perceptions of you and your work. Some things you can do straightaway such as change your clothes and become more involved in community or work activities. Other things need planning such as training courses or courses in improved communication or assertiveness. But do not leave it too late. You can use those new skills now while you are waiting for an opportunity to use them in a new area. But if you wait too late you may be passed over for that job you wanted if you haven't learnt the necessary skills.

Who's watching?

Keeping in the public eye is a necessary part of maintaining your image. You should be speaking to your professional association, writing letters to the media and articles for the trade press. You should be taking opportunities to speak in public and improve your communication skills. You should be offering your services when a volunteer from work is needed to meet the public. These things may be time-consuming but the public is fickle. If you don't keep in the news then you will soon be forgotten.

Winning in the workplace

To keep your new image intact in the eyes of your staff, colleagues and employers you need to work at it. If you are hardworking and innovative one week and sloppy and boring the next then you will not be held in high esteem – nor by association will be the work you do.

You must make sure that you always deliver work of the highest standard on time and that you have opinions and ideas to offer at work. Keep in touch with the latest thinking on your subject by reading books and magazines. If you always appear to be on the ball and willing to have a go at what you are asked to do you will be kept in mind as someone who is interested in the work and has ability. Office politics does play a part; you must be seen to be good and be heard to be enthusiastic and full of ideas. And you must be seen and heard doing this by the right people at the right time. If yours is the first name people think of when they think of the sales section or the PR section then you are on your way. Just make sure it is on people's minds for the right reason.

181

Enhancing opportunities

Opportunities can pass you by unless you know how to make the best of them. You must be on continual look-out for chances to show your worth and to be available when needed. Remember these things:

1 Be enthusiastic about your work to everyone
2 Volunteer for work or activities which will bring you into contact with your seniors

3 Learn how to communicate clearly in spoken and written speech and do so at all times

4 Don't complain about too much work; think of ways to reorganise or delegate it

5 Always do your best work

6 Being pleasant to people pays, but don't ignore the less senior staff

7 Don't associate with people you know will be disapproved of by most reasonable people

8 Be ready to take on an exciting opportunity – don't say 'I can't do that until next week'

9 Prepare thoroughly so that you can answer awkward questions about your work

10 Appear confident

11 Dress appropriately

Preparation is a key word here. You must be ready to seize exciting opportunities. It is no good saying, 'but I didn't know that' or 'I haven't learnt that'. You must have prepared for power in advance so that you don't have to waste time getting on in the job.

Casing the competition

Your colleagues can be your greatest allies or your worst enemies. You need to be able to get on well with them and command their respect. At the same time they may be after that same job.

While you are working with your colleagues you can be assessing them as opposition. What do other people admire about them? Is it something you could do? What irritated other people about them? Do you do it too? Can you change? By learning about your colleagues you can assess how well you can compete with them if necessary. Of course it is more difficult to assess the opposition from outside the company unless you have met them. You may find people who know them and can ask about them. Otherwise you must use your brains.

When a job opportunity comes up read the job description carefully to see how it fits you. The sit down and work out exactly what *you* would expect the person doing the job to be able to do and what qualities to expect. Compare the two lists. What is the same on both lists? Those are the most important things. What are the others? Can you do them? Or try for them? Or find out the necessary information in time? You can use this kind of analysis for head-hunting operations too.

Follow up your ten-day plan

After following your ten-day plan you should be well on your way to improving your image and raising the profile of both your work and yourself with everybody. What do you do when the ten days are up?

Use the plan as a review reminder. Every month read the plan through and see if there are any points you can improve on or which you haven't given enough attention to.

183

Use it with a colleague or friend. Both of you can follow the same day for the plan and then see how each of you has improved. Compare progress and work out which ideas suit you best. Be encouraging rather than negative in your comments to each other. If you think that you are slipping then follow the ten-day plan all over again. You can only improve and each time you will come up with more ideas.

LEARNING POINTS CHECKLIST

1 Your reputation is hard won and easily lost

2 Review your image regularly

3 Be positive about your progress

4 Don't make changes too late to be useful

5 Keep an eye on what your employers will want in the future

6 Don't ignore the people you work with

7 Be ready to take advantage of opportunities

8 Assess the competition

9 Use the ten-day plan as a review reminder

10 Follow the ten-day plan with a friend

Useful addresses

■

Institute of Management Cottingham Road, Corby NN17 1TT

Management News 3rd floor, 2, Savoy Court, Strand, London WC2R OEZ Tel: 071-240 2032

Management Services 1, Cecil Court, London Road, Enfield, EN2 6DD Tel: 0274 499 821 Fax: 0274 547 143

Management Today 22, Lancaster Gate, London W2 3LY Tel: 071-413 4566 Fax: 071-413 4138

National Institute of Adult Continuing Education 19b, De Montfort Street, Leicester, LE1 7GE Tel: 0533 551451

The Open University Learning Materials Sales Office, PO box 188, Milton Keynes, MK7 6DH

Wardrobe 3, Grosvenor Street, London W1 Tel:071-629 7044 or 17, Chiltern Street, London W1 Tel: 071-935 4086

Workers Educational Association (WEA) Temple House, 9, Upper Berkeley Street, London W1H 8BY

Further reading

■

P. Bartram: *How to write a Press Release* (How To Books, 1993)

Benns Media Directory

M. Bland, and S. Mondesir: *Promoting Yourself on TV and Radio* (Kogan Page, 1987).

Dr S. Blotnick: *The Corporate Steeplechase* (Facts on File, NY, 1994)

R.N. Bolles: *What Colour Is Your Parachute?* (Ten Speed Press, CA, 1987)

British Rate and Data (BRAD)

C. Cooper, and P. Hingley: *The Change Makers* (Harper & Row, 1985)

A. Crofts: *Hype!* (Hutchinson Business Books, 1990)

P. Davies: *Your total Image* (Piatkus, 1990)

P. Davies: *Personal Power* (Piatkus, 1991)

L. Fairbrother: *Your Message and the Media* (Nicholas Brealey, 1993)

S. Faux, with P. Davies: *Wardrobe* (Piatkus, 1988)

R. Haywood: *All About Public Relations* (McGraw Hill, 1991)

R.B. Irving: *When You are the Headline: Managing a Major News Story* (Dow-Jones Irwin, 1987)

C. Jackson: *Colour me Beautiful* (Piatkus, 1989)

B. Jaques: *The Colour and Style File* (Piatkus, 1989)

F. Jefkins: *Marketing and PR Media Planning* (Pergamon Press, 1974)

M. Jennings: *10 Steps to the Top* (Piatkus, 1992)

M. Jones: *Using the media* (NCVO Publications, 1992)

D. Leeds: *Marketing Yourself* (Piatkus, 1991)

M.H. McCormack: *What They don't Teach You in Harvard Business School* (Fontana/Collins, 1984)

G. Moss: *Getting your Ideas across* (Kogan Page, 1993)

A. Naylor: *Superlife: the Seven Steps that Spell Success* (Thorsons, 1993)

M. Peel: *Successful Presentation in a Week* (Hodder & Stoughton, 1992)

B. Penn: *Be your own PR Expert* (Piatkus, 1993)

D. Pooser: *Always in Style* (Piatkus, 1993)

R.H. Schuller: *You can Become the Person You want to be* (Pillar Books, NY, 1973)

M. Serif: *How to Manage Yourself* (Frederick Fell, NY, 1980)

Time To Learn, National Institute of Adult Continuing Learning (yearly)

D. Treacy: *Successful Time Management* (Hodder & Stoughton, 1993)

Willings Press Guide

Writers' and Artists' Yearbook (A & C Black, yearly)

Writers' Handbook, ed. B. Turner (Macmillan, yearly)

Index

■